STRAIGHT WIVES:
SHATTERED LIVES
VOLUME 2

TRUE STORIES OF WOMEN
MARRIED TO GAY & BISEXUAL MEN

COMPILED AND EDITED BY
BONNIE KAYE, M.Ed.

CCB Publishing
British Columbia, Canada

Straight Wives: Shattered Lives Volume 2
True Stories of Women Married to Gay & Bisexual Men

Copyright © 2011 by Bonnie Kaye, M.Ed.
ISBN-13: 978-1-926918-83-9
First Edition

Library and Archives Canada Cataloguing in Publication

Kaye, Bonnie, 1951-
Straight wives : shattered lives : volume 2 : true stories of women married to gay &
bisexual men / compiled and edited by Bonnie Kaye. – 1st ed.
ISBN 978-1-926918-83-9
Also available in electronic format.
1. Bisexuality in marriage.
2. Gay men--Relations with heterosexual women.
3. Closeted gays--Family relationships.
4. Marital conflict.
5. Wives--Biography. I. Kaye, Bonnie, 1951-
HQ1035.S773 2011   306.872   C2011-905983-5

Front Cover an original work of art by Maureen Kavaney Tillman:
http://MaureenTillman.blogspot.com   and   http://MaureenTillman.etsy.com

Publisher: CCB Publishing
               British Columbia, Canada
               www.ccbpublishing.com

Dedication

This book is dedicated to the millions of
women who live their lives in darkness.

There is light at the end of the tunnel.

Let the stories of our sisters in pain
help you find your way into the light.

Other books by Bonnie Kaye

The Gay Husband Checklist for Women Who Wonder

Over the Cliff: Gay Husbands in Straight Marriages

Doomed Grooms: Gay Husbands of Straight Wives

Man Readers: A Woman's Guide to Dysfunctional Men

Straight Wives: Shattered Lives (Volume 1)

Bonnie Kaye's Straight Talk

How I Made My Husband Gay: Myths About Straight Wives

and

La Lista de Control para Esposos Gay
Y Para Mujeres Que se Preguntan

Spanish edition of
The Gay Husband Checklist for Women Who Wonder

Contents

Introduction

When the first edition of Straight Wives: Shattered Lives was published in 2006, the response and reviews from women from around the world was overwhelmingly favorable with words that included, "life saving," "validating," "eye-opening," and "ground-breaking." This was the first book of its kind where women from five continents told true stories about their marriages to gay men. All of the stories were different as far as the names and places—but the emotional impact from each woman was universal and the same. So many women were able to clarify their own doubts and denial after reading this book.

Over the past five years, thousands of new women have come to me with their heartbreaking stories. I thought it is now time to do Part 2 of this book with other women who are willing to share their stories knowing how affirming it is to hear the words and experiences of others traveling this journey. In fact, several of women who contributed to this book stated they did so because of the impact they felt after reading the original stories.

I co-authored a new book titled "Over the Cliff: Gay Men in Straight Marriages" published in June of 2011 which was written in a similar format with married gay men telling their stories and struggles. I felt it was important for gay husbands to be able to connect to others who are struggling by living a daily lie in order for them to realize the importance of coming out to their wives which is ALWAYS my ultimate goal. In the book I told the men readers what I tell all men who come to me for help: if you truly love your wife, you owe her the real truth about why your marriage is failing. When you see the agonizing pain that our women face daily throughout the years in their marriages, you can understand why this missing piece of information is the key to solving the puzzle.

The problem with a number of married gay men is that they look to place the blame of the unhappiness in their marriages everywhere except where it belongs—which is on their homosexuality. You will see in some of these stories how husbands "externalize" the problem rather than internalize it. "If only you cleaned the house better, if only you didn't gain weight, if only you didn't spend so much time with the children…." I say if only, if only, if only…then what? He wouldn't be gay? These feelings wouldn't surface in his lifetime? He wouldn't have needed to find comfort in the arms or bed of another man? **Uhhh---I think not.**

I have studied homosexuality for three decades. I believe that people are born gay. They have no choice in their sexuality. No one would "choose" to be gay if they could "choose" to be straight. What would be the purpose? Sadly, no studies have provided a magical or even logical answer of why some gay men are able to deny their homosexuality for years while others can't at all. No one can explain why some gay men can perform adequate sex with a woman for a number of years while others shudder at the thought and could never do it. There are so many variables that have no rational or logical answer.

Some professionals explain this by making up "scales" like those of Kinsey in order to explain the differences away. Kinsey defines people on seven levels ranging from exclusively heterosexual to exclusively homosexual. Along the scale there are other choices. Some gay men love this scale because they feel so much better saying they are on the second level of the Kinsey scale (predominantly heterosexual but more than incidentally homosexual) than on the fourth level of the scale (predominantly homosexual but more than incidentally heterosexual). Like what is that? Why do we have to keep gay men in a bigger state of confusion and denial than they are already in?

As I tell my women, I have the Bonnie Kaye Scale of Sexuality. There are two levels on the scale. The first level is you are straight because you only want a woman. The second level says you are gay because you are thinking, fantasizing, viewing, or touching a penis. It doesn't matter if you have a wife and children or even if you're having sex with your wife. Here's my scientific formula:

Penis = Gay
Period!

Others believe that sexuality is fluid—moving through different phases as your life changes. There are theories of what causes homosexuality from the ridiculous to the more ridiculous including domineering mothers, passive fathers, absentee fathers, sexual molestation in childhood, bad role modeling, and the list goes on. I say who cares? Even if you don't believe that people are born gay, does it really matter how they became gay? It is what it is—and guess what? It doesn't matter because it isn't changing.

I know some wonderful gay men who have spent years and fortunes of money trying all kinds of therapies and medication to make them straight. It's a "No Go." In the end, they can't suppress their minds and bodies from the desire of wanting a man. There are also some men who are truly living in a limbo world—they desperately desire a straight life with a loving wife, but when it comes to sex—it is a man that excites them. They don't or won't or can't adapt to the gay world around them. Most likely they have been raised to hate what gay represents, so they stay in a world of denial justifying that it's just a physical act with a stranger. But they believe (or continue to convince themselves) that they are still straight—or like a famous exposed minister recently said about his own gay indiscretions, "I am straight with issues."

I gave up trying to argue with people about it being what it is—namely gay. I have people disputing me on a regular basis about my "black and white" views on the issue. After nearly 30 years and over 70,000 women, I feel qualified to say that this is black and white. I can't see the "grays"—only the "gays." If your man wants a man, fantasizes about a man sexually, looks at gay porno, thinks of men to sexually stimulate him when he performs with you, watches gay videos, well....call it what it is. GAY. I don't believe in different levels on the scale because to me, it's irrelevant. It doesn't matter if a man wants a man 10% of the time, 40% of the time, or 100% of the time. He wants a man. I wouldn't feel any better because my husband is thinking about men 25% of the time when he is making love to me. Well, for that matter—not even 1%. This is *not* what women want in a marriage.

As a side note, I know this book has the word "*bisexual*" in the subtitle. I don't want to mislead anyone. I don't believe in bisexuality. I believe it is a way that gay men make themselves feel better—or "straighter"--because they have a wife and children. By identifying with "bi," they don't have to say scary word "gay." I only put the word "bisexual" in the title because there are women who believe their husbands are bisexual. These are women who don't understand homosexuality—yet. The word "bi" misleads women into thinking there is a choice which gives them a false sense of hope. "If I love him hard enough, he will love me better and want me more than men because he has a choice." The joke is on them. It doesn't happen.

There are some women who will do anything to try to make their marriages work when they hear this news. This is the bargaining part of the grieving process. Trust me—I've been there and done that. Most of our women love their husbands and don't want to break up their marriages. They want to stay married to the men they fell in love with and built a life with. They don't want to become single parents and be responsible for raising and supporting a family primarily on their own.

At first, some women look to hang on to their gay husbands at any cost. You will read some of those stories in this book. In time they realize this is not what they bargained for when they said their wedding vows. They did agree to "for richer and for poorer, in sickness and in health." There was no mention of "for straight and for gay" anywhere in the vows. Some of our women in their desperation even "consider" making adjustments to their marriages by either allowing their husbands to see someone for sex or turning a blind eye as long as they don't have to know about it. In time, being an ostrich only works for so long. The marriage is doomed.

There are women come to me filled with hope. I'm not sure why. They know where I stand, but they keep thinking I'm holding back a precious nugget or two of possibilities for fixing the problem. These are mostly the women who had good and loving husbands, and they can't understand how everything changed so suddenly after a number of wonderful years of marriage. My heart goes out to these women. I always say it is more difficult to recover from losing a good marriage than from losing a bad one. I am the counselor that refuses to give false hope to any woman who is struggling with this issue. All I can give women hope for is that they can salvage a wonderful friendship and "readjust" their family expectations. I do believe you can still be a family even when you are no longer married if you have TWO willing participants.

What is so amazing is the prevalence of these marriages— encompassing millions of people throughout the world—and yet the isolation that each woman feels is equally universal. Each woman feels the same sense of horror leading her through a whole new myriad of problems that she is not equipped to deal with. This is not like other divorces where couples fall out of love. These are divorces that leave the wife feeling the ultimate state of betrayal and without a roadmap for her future. Trust me, the problems in the aftermath of straight/gay marriages are very different than others.

As you'll see in these stories, years of ongoing emotional deterioration and neglect—in and out of the bedroom—leave our women in a shattered state. They feel stripped of their dignity, sexuality, mental well being, and in many cases, sanity. This comes through a process that I refer to as "Gaylighting," which is similar to "Gaslighting." This is when the gay husband tries to make the wife feel that she is crazy because she knows the truth about him. These men are manipulative and they know how to push all the buttons of their already beaten-down wives who are living in a state of confusion and disconnect. A woman loses her sense of reality questioning what is real and not real. Her sense in her own judgment is hanging by a thread because her belief system is constantly being challenged and rebuffed. Even the strongest of women can easily lose themselves in a situation like this. I know—I was one of those women.

By connecting to other women, we have the opportunity of learning from others that what we are going through is "normal." All the fears, sickness, insecurity, and feelings of hopelessness are part of the process in moving ahead. And most importantly—it takes time. I tell gay husbands you struggled for a LIFETIME; don't expect your wife to "get over it" in a few weeks, months, or even sometimes years. There are so many factors involved. But we are strong women—and we do recover. Many of us have moved on and found true love—with straight men.

I hope after you read these stories, you'll start repeating my personal mantra daily:

<u>LIFE WAS NEVER MEANT TO BE THIS COMPLICATED!</u>
<u>PERIOD!</u>

I say period following that statement so you won't think there is room for widening the space with words such as, "well maybe," "if only," or "what if." Those words are "time wasters in your life." They delay what is as you'll see in the beautiful stories that follow.

Special Thanks

A note of extra special thanks goes to Maureen Kavaney Tillman who designed the beautiful cover for this book. Maureen is a remarkable artist, and I love brightening up my home with the beautiful art objects I've found on her site. You can see and purchase her artwork on her websites at:

http://MaureenTillman.blogspot.com
http://MaureenTillman.etsy.com

Maureen contributed these heartfelt words to our book about her own personal experience with her marriage:

Maureen's Story

Having a bad day…
Note to self: Never again watch the movie, "The Notebook".

It's not like it was the first time I ever watched it, yet I was overcome with sadness and tears. It was the recognition that if just as in the movie, I was an Alzheimer's sufferer who had only five precious minutes of lucidity everyday to relive treasured memories of true love, I would still be bereft. For as I do hold memories, I learned they do not reflect the reality of my life, the true knowledge of which was denied to me all those many years. In retrospect, my life turned out to be all smoke and mirrors. So there would be no moments of lucidity, no redemptive memories, no insight, no whole truth now or ever. Just questions of which I would never be given the satisfactory answers although I know they exist. For me there would only be denial…endless denial.

My life, my reality for four decades was solely someone else's invention. What I believed to be love all those years was a lie. The occasional small expressions of love were the cruel empty words of a liar. I was wed under false pretenses with a fraudulent vow of a love that could never be simply because I was a woman. Just weeks into our marriage in his only moment of truth to me ever, he said we were doomed simply because we got married. I now understand what it was he meant. We never had a chance. Tragically I never had a chance. I just never knew it until it was all over. My life as I knew it was over, my life as I knew it never existed.

The price his long deception extracted from me, his secret slow shakedown that almost bled my spirit dry staggered my belief and trust in my own knowing, my own perception of truth and reality. And it convinced me that real love is very rare and everything else is less than, even undesirable and threatening.

Today I also struggle with the slow lingering dying of my father, the abusive monster of my early life who now although withered and decrepit in body can still wound me with his vicious hateful words. Never to be the father I needed, the one who loved me unconditionally and made me understand that I was good and lovable as a child, his mantra for me now has become, "I have to love you, I don't have to like you!"

Too young a bride, I married a man who I believed would rescue me-- not seeing he was just a mere confused and frightened boy himself in search of his own rescue, his own life of denial. I trusted he was the man of my dreams, both those childhood dreams of rescue by the handsome brave knight riding the magnificent white steed that protected me until sleep came; and also the dreams of desperation for being loved, feeling loved, and even more vital feeling lovable. But slowly under the false security of a false marriage, all those dreams disintegrated along with my sense of self-worth. Imperceptibly during that same period denial slowly supplanted my marriage contract and became my way of life.

My vow became a spiritual promise to preserve my soul's blindness so as not to see the truth. To live in denial, too stubborn, too desperate to see there was no love there, to see the man behind the mask had never loved me, nor found me to be lovable. He couldn't. I was a woman - but a woman with a child's heart destined to be broken irreparably.

Anne's Story

Although Zeke and I knew each other in high school, we weren't particularly close and didn't stay in touch after graduation. In our mid-twenties, we discovered we were living in the same town and instantly became close friends. Although I didn't have any physical attraction to him, we started dating, felt like soul-mates, and couldn't imagine not being together.

The first night we spent together, he told me that he had had a couple of experiences with men that had not been heavily sexual. While I was concerned about it, I also knew he had had a couple of long-term girlfriends, and had mentioned several women for whom his very strong feelings had been unrequited. During our year-long courtship, and not infrequently after being married, it was obvious to me that there were women he was sincerely attracted to. He wasn't faking it for my benefit-- in fact, he tried to hide it, but I could tell when he had that certain kind of giddy nervousness.

Over the next 15 years together, I could count at least a dozen women, but only one man that I could tell he was attracted to. Nevertheless, problems with our physical relationship from the very beginning, plus my lurking concerns about his sexuality, led me to insist that we see a marital therapist before going forward with a wedding that was being planned. Although he was never willing to talk about sexuality per se, the physical relationship improved enough that, with some trepidation, I went forward with the wedding.

It was always clear to me that Zeke loved me as much as any woman could every want. Why, he could have been described as a model husband and, once the children began coming, a model father, as well. Nevertheless, the physical relationship was perfunctory, mechanical, lacking in passion, devoid of kissing, and often avoided due to being too tired, too full, feeling fat, etc. And while Zeke never treated me badly in ways that so many other women report, I have often wondered whether his undercurrent of anger and neediness grow out of repressed homosexuality. As Bonnie would say, it's hard to fight anger if it's due to my not having a penis.

By the time the third child came along, I had pretty much lost any interest in sex anyway, so 5 minutes most weeks was okay with me. I put on a bit of weight (going from perhaps a size 8/10 to 12/14) and rarely felt attractive to, or attracted by other men-- until I met Chris. One spring, I developed an immense crush on a guy that I encountered at an office retreat. While it seemed clear that the feelings were mutual, it also seemed clear that he wasn't going to act on it. Needless to say, my libido awoke from its decade-plus slumber.

The very night I returned from the trip, Zeke asked me to help him get his computer connected to the internet—a not infrequent request. After fiddling with various settings, I launched a browser to see whether I succeeded. When my cursor hovered over the address bar, the history showed up and my stomach lurched. While there was nothing pornographic or overtly gay, I was deeply alarmed at what I saw. I called him downstairs and confronted him as soon as the kids were in bed. Looking like a caged rat, he said he had no explanation— that he hadn't acted on such desires—but couldn't tell me why he was doing what he was doing. However, I felt horribly hypocritical reaming him out while feeling like I had just committed emotional infidelity.

I asked myself, "Is his enjoyment of looking at male actors' head shots really worse than my having actual feelings for an actual person?" I felt rather tormented as I spent every waking moment asking myself whether I would actually have an affair with Chris, should the opportunity present itself. Once again, I insisted that we pursue therapy. I disclosed my own near infidelity to him, perhaps hoping to impress upon him just how serious of a threat I took "the discovery" to be. In retrospect, by disclosing my own crush (and even who it was, as Zeke knew him from a recreational activity), I think I was trying to diffuse the sexuality issue in hopes that he would drop his defensiveness enough to meaningfully engage with a therapist.

We went to a highly regarded sex therapist who promised that, by the end of a course of therapy with her, she was confident that we'd have the best sex ever. However, he barely went through the motions of fulfilling her requirement of at least 8 weekly sessions. Needless to say, the more he refused to open up, the more concerned I became. During this time, I found Bonnie. Although I did not embrace her view that there is no such thing as bisexuality, her personal words to me, and the stories of her readers were enormously enlightening and comforting.

The failure of therapy left me terribly depressed. I had always thought, in the back of my mind, that perhaps a skilled sex therapist would be able to help us. That hope was then dashed forever. In the mean time, sporadic (chaste) encounters with Chris stoked my crush. Between a revved metabolism (I calculated that a crush like that burned 300 calories/day) and a sudden desire to work out, I got in the best shape of my life. A therapist I continued to consult from time to time on my own commented, "If the dramatic change in your appearance didn't generate a reaction from your husband, nothing will." That remark burned in my ears and I soon found myself developing feelings for virtually every man I encountered, or so it seemed. When a close friend, in a loveless marriage, told me that she was having an affair, I thought, "Damn it—why can't I do that?" I recalled the bargain that I made with my maker when marrying Zeke: because our relationship felt divinely inspired: I would marry him but retain the right to have an affair if the physical relationship didn't improve. After three children, 15 years of marriage and two failed rounds of therapy, I felt entitled.

Aside from my continuing obsession with Chris, who I encountered frequently at work, I felt myself falling for Greg who, together with his wife, was among our very closest friends. Although it seemed that Greg, too, had feelings for me, I knew that I could not act on it (and doubted he would, either). Somehow, I stumbled on personal ads for married people and decided that it would be safer to seek a no-strings-attached affair with a stranger than risk destroying a lot of lives by falling in love with a married friend or colleague.

Over the course of several months, I began exchanging messages with men I met online, seeking someone who was committed to his own marriage, hadn't done this before, and shared my need for complete secrecy. I soon found that it's a "buyer's market" for women in this world! There must have been 200 men for every woman looking, and was it ever a different experience to feel like I could call all of the shots! And I did. After meeting a number of men for a drink or coffee and almost always being the one to opt out of further interaction, I met John—whose wife had refused sex since the birth of their second child nearly a decade before. We went very slowly, but after a number of "dates," had an afternoon in a hotel that felt like I gave myself the honeymoon I never had. "How could your husband lie next to you every night and not want to have sex with you all night long?" he asked. Wow!

After several months, I grew concerned that John was starting to want more and talking about ending his marriage when his child left the house in a year or two. At my preference, we ended the relationship but have remained friends. That "starter affair" taught me that, not only was I capable of pulling it off, but in many ways, I felt like I was a better wife and mother because I was taking care of myself. So I began the search again, adding a few more rigorous "selection criteria" to weed out anyone I felt might fall in love with me. And, despite feeling rather unloved at home, I rejected a lot of prospective suitors for that reason! As I got better at weeding people out, I also took great comfort in the process. I realized just how desirable I was, and how many men would kill for a wife who was actually interested in having an active sexual relationship. I heard so many heart-breaking stories of men who were doing exactly what I was doing--straying in hopes of keeping the marriage together. Lord knows, no one seeking an exit strategy from their marriage would do so by finding a partner on websites that specialize in adultery! After many more months of looking, I found Elliot. I was so attracted to him that I ached for him, and even after a year of seeing him, trembled at the anticipation of being together. However, the relationship became rocky when we had difficulty getting schedules to mesh…and perhaps we were both concerned about getting in deeper than either of us wanted and it ended about two years ago.

Since then, I've gotten more concerned about the impossibility of assuring security with internet dating. It seems to me that the proliferation of facial recognition software precludes exchanging photos with prospective partners, and IP addresses are too easily extracted from emails. (I should know—I was easily able to determine the identities of a significant fraction of men I corresponded with.) I struggled mightily with whether or not to remain married, but a family move during this time, plus some severe difficulties with one of my children, complicated matters. In our former town, it would have been possible to leave the marriage but still see my kids every day. Now, splitting up would mean my moving away without the kids and I couldn't fathom that. Hard work with a therapist, coupled with the collective wisdom that Bonnie has so graciously shared through her newsletters over the years has led me to several very helpful insights:

The affairs confirmed to me that the sex with my husband was as inadequate as I thought it was. After all those years of being angry with him for not providing the physical companionship I wanted, I realized that I had no desire for him whatsoever and was just as happy to be left alone.

Desire begets desire—it's possible that my lack of desire is in part a response to not feeling desired by him. Or, it may be that I feel revulsion toward a man who is attracted to men. Same difference in the end!

Whether or not my husband is gay really doesn't matter. What does matter is that my needs are not being met.

Even though I had suspicions that my husband might be gay from the very beginning, I had every reason to hope that our physical relationship would improve. Even had I known exactly what I was getting into, I would be justified in leaving a marriage that is virtually devoid of a physical element.

As I'm not in a position to leave now, I am trying to allow myself to enjoy the many wonderful aspects that are in our relationship. And, while I know that staying in a marriage like this can be a mixed bag for the children, in my case, I think they are far better off with us together and splitting up would be near disastrous for them. And, the sincere love we have for one another is not something to discard. In some ways, it seems like having one or the other of us fall in love with someone else would be the best end game. I sometimes wish that my husband would actually fall in love with a man and allow himself to explore what may (or may not) be his authentic self.

I hope there will be another book in five years, and that I'll have a different story to tell. But for now, I am somewhat at peace with having taken matters into my own hands within certain constraints. But mostly, I want to express my immense gratitude to Bonnie for saving so many of us—and doing so as a volunteer. When I first wrote her, she might as well have said, "Okay, the 32,167[th] letter from a woman who thinks her husband will be the first one who is truly bisexual. She'll write me again within a year-or two or ten when she realizes that a man who desires men cannot give a woman what she needs and deserves." Well Bonnie, you were right, and I hope that having my story to share makes your job just a little bit easier.

Anne wanted me to update our readers with a P.S. written several months after she submitted this story:

Two months ago, I changed jobs to work in a nearby city. With my eldest leaving home in the fall, I started letting myself envision being able to live separately but still work and see my kids. This past week, I went by myself to an acting camp of sorts and wound up having a very intense week of being profoundly moved by being on stage, feeling my joy be unlocked, having very instantaneous and meaningful connections with others, and came to a realization--through many tears, that I must lead an authentic life. I realized how completely shut down I had become and that my joy had been locked away.

When I got home, I told my husband that I would not sit across from him in a couple of weeks and "celebrate" our 20th anniversary without each of us understanding what kind of marriage each other was in. He gave me an opening as he had just relayed a conversation he had had with a good friend who lamented how she and her husband spend all of their time alone in their separate studies. I told him that I had gone to my study seven years ago and wondered whether he even knew that. In being home for a week and reading/talking to people, I realized that what happened to me last week was that I became "enlightened" in the spiritual sense. I was not looking for that and it wasn't part of camp. I just happened. I connected very profoundly with others including a man 20 years my junior... perhaps because he was "safe" in comparison with other men who were on their own at camp. I became able to step away from my life and understand it in ways that seem to make about 5 years of therapy (that I've had cumulatively over the last 30 years) be accessible to me.

At any rate, I don't know where this is leading, but the road I was on just made a 90 degree turn, and I am liking the new view!

Di's Story

I never thought this would happen to me in a million years

The apprehension and nervousness I feel in writing my story equals the nausea I still feel in relation to this whole experience. My heart is pounding and I feel quite emotional. But I'd like to share my experience with others so that they can maybe realize that they are not alone in this surreal, heart breaking experience.

These are my thoughts and experiences from my perception. Of course, my ex-husband and possibly his family may feel differently. After our divorce I was told that our marriage was failing anyway. I disagree. Of course it was going to fail eventually. I became the "problem" in our relationship. I was straight. No matter what I did it wasn't going to be right. Of course resentment is going to occur after time and this is quite evident in our relationship and my story.

I'd like to share some of my key experiences with you. Isn't hindsight such a wonderful thing? There were so many signs that I missed about his true identity. I will try to share with you some signs and behaviors that should send you a red flag if you are in doubt your husband is controlling, manipulative and probably gay.

I met my Anthony in 1991, when I was 21 and he was 24. He was a Preschool Teacher and I was an Instrumental Teacher. I was raised by my grandparents and still living at home. I had little prior experience with dating and having boyfriends. I wasn't the typical teenager dating a lot of guys, and I had high morals. I felt that I was attractive, slim, and dressed very stylishly but just felt that I hadn't met the right person. Anthony's Teacher Aide introduced us, and she thought that we could be well suited. Anthony asked me on a date the day after my 22nd birthday. It all seemed so natural. He was easy to be around and I just felt that we clicked. He told me that he'd never had a girlfriend before because he, too, hadn't met the right person. Naively, I thought, "Okay, he's just like me." Three months into the relationship I knew that he was "the one." He seemed to be what I was looking for, a "New Age Guy." He was dressed well, mannerly, educated, immaculate in the house and a great cook. What more could I want?

While we were dating, he shared a unit with another male teacher from his school. I would stay overnight usually mid-week and on weekends. We were young and I enjoyed the intimacy of a new relationship. One night when I stayed over he said to me, "We don't have to have sex every time you stay over." I did think that was unusual for a guy to say when we were at the beginning of a relationship. Don't most guys like to have sex at least twice a week? And preferably more? Anthony was always sweet and was able to justify everything. On a few occasions, he became impotent. I couldn't understand why. Once again, he would say, "This happens sometimes," and I would just accept it. How would I know with my lack of experience?

We were engaged in 1993 and married in 1994. It was a big change for me as I lived at home until the wedding. Sometime prior to the wedding, Anthony rang me very upset. I couldn't work out the problem. He just wasn't making any sense. He argued with my Grandmother, but I stood by him. What was the problem? Understandably, I became emotional. When he heard the pain and anguish in my voice he seemed to settle down. It's not until this very moment that it makes real sense. He was trying to find an excuse to get out of the wedding but wasn't going to admit that he was gay. As the story goes on, you'll see a pattern of blaming others rather than admitting the real issue.

Our wedding was beautiful and a day that I will always cherish. Anthony was always a confident person; I was the shy one. But during our vows, Anthony stumbled on his words. For a person used to speaking in front of an audience, this was unusual. I justified it by saying it must be just the nerves. Yet, I said my vows fluently, confidently, and proudly. I was so happy to be marrying him, how lucky I am! The priest didn't say, "You can kiss the bride." Anthony was so nervous he must not have realized that it was time to kiss me. So I said, "You can kiss me." He pecked me on the lips, and we were married. That night, I was so run down from the wedding and unwell I actually didn't care if we were intimate or not. Anthony didn't seem to care either. But tradition says that's what you do. By the way, Anthony never commented on how beautiful I looked that day.

I thought our reception was wonderful, everything I had dreamed of. Anthony, on the other hand, found fault in the service at the reception. Years later, he still complained about the service. I remembered the wedding fondly whilst he found fault in it. Perhaps this was another clue. He knew that he was dishonest to both himself and me. This brings me to honesty. Anthony always made such a big deal about being honest. I always thought he was the most honest person I knew. He even spoke about people having affairs and how our marriage wouldn't last if either of us had one. It didn't cross my mind that either one of us would do that. We were both honest, trustworthy, and genuine people-- or so I thought!.

The first time I thought that there was something wrong with Anthony was just after our first wedding anniversary. I had been studying at the conservatorium of Music. Anthony said that we needed to move closer to his work which was too far for me to commute. I was going to have to give up my studies. I was devastated. I had finally found a place that I felt at "home" and was with like minded people. I cried at night for three months anguishing over my decision. Anthony never comforted me during these times. When I asked him why he didn't comfort me he would reply, "Oh, maybe because my stepmother used to cry, and I just turn off from it." In the end, I decided that the sacrament of marriage was more important to me, so I gave up the conservatorium and moved away. This was the first of many sacrifices during our marriage.

I should mention that Anthony was the one that persuaded me to study. Although I had been teaching music since I was 15, I didn't have a Tertiary Qualification. He was always thinking and planning for the future. He told me that I should have a formal qualification because there are benefits. Yes, he was very thoughtful--or manipulative! I believe he knew what he was doing from the beginning of our relationship. He wanted to be married and have two boys. He didn't want girls; he wouldn't know what to do with them! His wish came true. We did have two boys.

Our first son was born in 1997. Sadly, he was born with a major congenital heart defect which was naturally, very distressing. He spent the first four months of his life in and out of hospital with infections. Anthony struggled to cope with all the problems associated with a distressing birth then the aftermath of caring for a sick baby. Anthony helped with practical things such as washing the nappies or getting the baby's bottles sanitized. He just wasn't very good with the everyday care or giving me a break to catch up on sleep. He said that he had to work and couldn't cope if he didn't have his sleep. I was worn out. What about me? Oh, of course, that didn't matter. I wasn't the type of person to yell and scream; rather, I just accepted it. Since my divorce, a close friend of mine said, "He's narcissistic and abused your good will and nature throughout your marriage." I tend to agree, but at the time however, I would have denied this emphatically.

Anthony struggled with the demands of being the sole financial provider. He began calling me a liability, it was very hurtful behavior. In my mind, most fathers went to work to provide for their family while the wife stayed home with the baby. The first time I can really distinguish that Anthony seemed distant was at the birth of our second son. I should admit that he also didn't seem very caring during my pregnancy. Let's say, he didn't lavish me with a lot of attention or affection – "pregnancy is natural, it's not an illness." I had literally just given birth and asked him for a kiss. He pecked me on the lips without any emotion. I was looking for comfort, reassurance and just wanted to share this beautiful moment with my husband.

When our son was 10 weeks old, I suffered appendicitis. We were visiting friends in another town for the weekend when this happened. I couldn't believe it. Anthony didn't care for the baby during the nights, but rather he let our friend care for him. She already had four children and they worked on a farm. Our friend was exhausted by the time I got out of hospital. Why didn't Anthony care for the baby? That's right, he needed his sleep! On the long drive home, Anthony began discussing where we could live. His thoughts were irrational. In one moment he said he'd like to live on acreage, to the next living near the ocean in a unit. Perhaps this was the beginning of his mental illness surfacing.

I haven't mentioned to you that Anthony liked to move regularly. We would just get settled and then he wanted to move on. He would justify this by saying, "Only stagnant teachers stayed at the one school." By this stage, Anthony had been promoted to Deputy Principal. I found the moves very traumatic. I had lived at home for my entire life prior to our wedding. A pattern developed--he wanted to move every three years. I figured this was to hide his true identity. Once people became too close he wanted to put distance into the relationship. Anthony wanted to move us a long distance from my family because he felt that their ties were too strong. But the last time he asked me to move I finally got the courage to say, "I'm not moving even if this costs our marriage."

I wanted a home for our family. Anthony always thought of it as a house, merely a possession. I tried to explain to him how important it was for me to establish a secure home for the boys. But Anthony always spoke of renovating our house with future intentions of selling. He already knew his plan. On the last occasion, he wanted to down size our home so that we could have a more comfortable style of living. I actually think that he wanted to move me hours away from my family to isolate me and then eventually, leave me. Or perhaps this was his last attempt at trying to hold his life/lie together, I'm not sure.

In 2003, Anthony had a breakdown. I believe that I was very caring and nurturing to him during this time. It was very difficult to maintain a "normal" life when you're on suicide watch with two children in the house. He couldn't cope with the noise of the boys, and I had to keep them away from him. He virtually stayed in bed for the first three months. As time went on, he began smoking (he hadn't smoked since before meeting me) and drinking. He referred to it as "self medication." I attended many appointments with the psychologist and psychiatrist trying to establish why he had a breakdown and how to manage it and move forward. At one stage I even asked him if he could be gay. I thought that perhaps as he wasn't the typical macho guy, and maybe he struggled with his sexuality. He denied this emphatically!

We still weren't having sex, but I put this down to the depression and low libido. As time went on, the psychiatrist couldn't understand why he still had a low libido and prescribed him with Viagra. On a few occasions we attempted to be intimate after he took the Viagra, but it wasn't successful. He convinced me that there wasn't anything wrong so once again, I just put it down to depression. During this time I continued my studies part time. Anthony had always wanted me to finish my degree. In hindsight, I now understand that he wanted me to have a formal qualification so that I could be totally independent and he could move on with his life.

In 2007, Anthony began working part time in a new career path. He was beginning to get back on his feet and things were beginning to look up, or so I thought. During stages of Anthony's depression we seemed to be very close. We often sat up through the night just talking and working through Anthony's "stuff." I thought that we were bonding once again. During this time he was given testosterone injections which seemed to elevate his mood. Anthony said that this doctor was wonderful, he'd never felt better. So, if the testosterone was more balanced, wouldn't he want to be intimate with his wife? Well, no. I did think this was a little unusual but figured he'd had a mental illness for almost four years and that it would all balance out eventually.

As the year progressed, Anthony's mood swings turned to anger and frustration. He showed signs of being in a "high" state which was just the opposite of his depression. Anthony became emotional one day and said to me, "I don't want to cheat." I thought this was bizarre. I was here, waiting to be his wife again, why would he want to cheat? Soon after, I thought that I would assist him by initiating sex. He said that he was busy in the office, but he would come to bed soon. Time passed, and I came to check on him. Finally, he gave in and we had sex. He said to me, "that's the best sex we've had." I replied, "Well, perhaps we're reconnecting." Something felt different though. That was the last time we were intimate.

Towards the end of 2007, Anthony was becoming more and more aggravated and upset. He blamed me for everything. I didn't clean well, I bought too much take away, I'd got fat, and I was useless. One day, he terrified me. He had never been like this. He was yelling and screaming and I actually felt threatened. As usual, I justified it by saying it's the bipolar. Nevertheless, I was so fearful that he may actually lose it that I hid at the back of the house and called the police. I then went to a neighbor's house for refuge. I was scared and upset. When things settled, Anthony said that he was going to visit his brother and leave for a while so that I could finish my last University assessments without the distraction. Where was his support again? Couldn't he help with the boys while I finished my studies? It had taken close to ten years to finish because of all the turmoil in our lives.

Finally, I finished my last exam and found out immediately that I had passed. I rang Anthony to let him know that I'd finished my degree. He began to cry. I said, "Don't cry honey, I finally did it." He said that he'd be home in a couple of days. I was very disappointed. He was the one that had encouraged me to do my degree, and yet he wasn't here to celebrate my achievement. He did send me flowers, which he often did during our marriage.

He came home a couple of days later. We were going out for coffee to celebrate my achievement. I thought, "Finally. We can put all this pain behind us and move on with our lives." I was very excited. I said to Anthony, "Come on, are we going?" He was busy in the office as usual. Eventually, he said he was ready. We drove not far from home and he pulled up on the side of the road.

He started with, "I don't know how to tell you this." So he gave me some medical forms about his illness. I glanced at it. It said "homosexuality." I said, "Yeah, okay," because I figured he was questioning himself in this area, not that he really is homosexual. But then he said it, "I'm homosexual and leaving. We'll never have sex again." What are you talking about? Then he handed me forms about a unit he had leased and who knows what else. I thought we were celebrating my achievement, but here he was telling me he's gay and leaving? I could never have imagined this. I thought we were together forever. We weren't the typical couple that fought. We had strong morals didn't we?

I was in shock. I managed to get out of the car and rang my sister. I said, "Anthony's gay and he's leaving". He drove me home. I was a mess. I saw the neighbor next door and said to him, "Did you know he's gay?" Poor guy. I came inside the house crying, distraught. I spoke to my eldest son who was ten and said, "Dad's leaving, he's gay". We were all crying then. Anthony got annoyed with me for sharing this news with our son. He wanted to have more plans in place to support the boys. I'm not sure how he thought he was going to achieve this.

In the next month or two we visited a counselor. He was gay himself and supported people coming out. He was very nice. However, we weren't just dealing with homosexuality. Anthony was on the high end of the bipolar. He began spending a lot of money. He was renting hotels that cost a fortune. Early on, he

24

even slept on a park bench overnight. He would rant and rave. You couldn't have a normal conversation with him. I was still trying to come to terms with it all. I met him with the boys in the city a couple of times. Anthony would say to people how well we got on--wasn't it wonderful? We were co-operative parents as he referred to it. Life is great!

I began receiving government payments during this period. I couldn't get my head around what was happening. Anthony seemed to hate me. He yelled and carried on because I took so long signing the contract and sharing our assets. It was only two months after he said he was gay. Fortunately, we did settle quickly because in a few months, Anthony had declared bankruptcy. The boys and I could have lost everything!

During this phase, Anthony came in contact with many people that would introduce him to his new life. He changed his appearance significantly. His hair was bleached blonde, and he got piercings and tattoos. He wore a completely different style of clothing and became extremely thin. As he was high with being bipolar, he was throwing money everywhere. Of course, there were a lot of leeches around him. Anthony spoke of people "teaching" him how to have gay sex. He had no respect for me at all, nor did he show an ounce of care. Stupidly, I allowed him to stay in our office with a male friend for a week because they had nowhere to go. I couldn't make sense what was happening, yet I was still trying to support him.

Three years later, he has settled down. He managed to work part time for a while and had a long term relationship that failed after two years. He is currently living with his mum and appears to be managing his bipolar condition. He has disassociated with his father and brother. His mental illness combined with his homosexuality has really impacted on his life, not to mention mine and our children. He's had difficulty working and balancing his life. We rarely talk and I try not to see him if possible, it's too distressing.

I have our children full time. The children visit their dad occasionally at their grandma's. It's been a struggle, and I'm still not over it. Each day is getting better. As with any grief, it takes time. I no longer get upset every minute or hour, half a day or even a full day. One day at a time and bit by bit the pain reduces. My pain is always just below the surface and behind my thoughts. I don't know whether I'll ever understand how a person could use another person this way then to betray them like that and later discard them. Anthony knew he was gay from the beginning. He told me that he knew he was different as a child. He also knew that he would leave one day after having a family. Instead of accepting his homosexuality, he chose to live another life, hurting me, his wife, and our children.

This was not a normal divorce. We didn't just drift apart or through natural consequences. Our lives were mapped out according to Anthony. I'm not really sure how to move forward. Each day is a struggle. I struggle financially and emotionally. I struggle that I have to work full time and can't be home even when the kids are sick because I can't afford a day off. I struggle with the loneliness and the betrayal. This is not the life I envisioned. We should have been enjoying a comfortable life style. We should have grown old together. Our family should be together. Sometimes I really miss him or perhaps I miss what I thought we had. All of my dreams have been shattered along with my heart. I regularly think, "How could he have done this to me?" The other phrase that goes through my mind regularly is, "I never thought this would have happened to me in a million years."

I get support from Bonnie's newsletters. Unfortunately, there aren't any support groups in my part of Australia. I've thought of starting up one myself but when do I have the time? I hope my story has made you feel that you are not alone. We have been betrayed, and I think that should be acknowledged. I continue to see a psychologist monthly to help me get through life. Do whatever it takes to get through this. I have not given up on love and hope to find real love one day. As of yet, I'm still alone. I rarely get any time to myself, let alone have time to date anyone. I have put on a lot of weight since I've had children, and I know this is a result of the emotional turmoil. Hopefully, I can get some balance in my life again one day and look forward to the future. At the moment, I'm still just getting by, but little by little it's getting easier.

PS. I found writing in a diary helped me to express my emotions. Here's a recent entry:

Today, I am lonely.
I miss him. I miss what was.
I miss my dreams. I miss sharing it with someone.
I feel alone. No one understands the enormous pain I feel.
I'm supposed to hate him for what he has done. And yes, sometimes I resent him, perhaps hate or despise him.
How could he do this to me? I was supposed to be the one he loved and yet he lied and abused my love and trust in him.
I was the innocent victim.
Where are my rights in all of this? Gay people want rights but why should mine be taken away by someone so selfish?
Why should our children suffer because of his inability to accept who he was? It's not fair on any of us.
My children want a Dad to be proud of yet, they are embarrassed. They don't have a Dad to take them to sports to share their interest. If they visit him, their lives must stop. They're embarrassed by their Dad, his lifestyle.
Perhaps they will come to accept it more in the future but why should they have to be in this position? Their dreams are shattered too. All children want is to have a safe, secure home with their Mum and Dad. Now it's been taken from them. Their lifestyle has also changed significantly. I can no longer afford luxuries, holidays or sometimes even simple things. But, this is not a necessity in life.
I hope that things will improve in the future. I hope to find someone for myself but for them too. A real man. A man that will show them another side to life, not just a Gay life! That may sound terrible but that's how I feel.

Underneath, I am not homophobic (isn't that one of the reasons he chose me in the first place?). I have had gay friends and have a gay brother. I've been to Gay venues. I'd accept my husband coming out one day, wouldn't I? The answer is NO!

I did not want to marry a Gay Man. How could anyone marry someone knowing that it would one day end in disaster? A very selfish person that's who!

Perhaps I should support gay rights more. Then, other people may not end up in this situation. If people feel free to come out then it may not impact on others. But I can't do this now or in the foreseeable future. But who knows?

Dollie's Story
Don't Ask, Don't Tell

Memoirs of a Straight Wife,
Whose Ex was a Lt. Colonel in the USAF

I am a member of a unique set of women who have been married to a gay man; perhaps not so unique, really, since there are millions of us. For me, after more than 27 years of marriage, I found out not by his admission, (I asked, and he lied), but through telephone records of his secret life.

On a daily basis, during my married life, I tried to cope with the craziness of living with a gay man. I did not know or understand the meaning of my pain. I was fighting a war of sanity – trying to remain sane in the face of insanity. For you see, nothing is what it seems in these marriages – lies and manipulation, verbal and emotional abuse are the name of this game. I was not educated at all about gay men; I never thought I had to be because who would have thought that a gay man would have any interest in a straight woman?

My ex-husband had been in the Air Force for almost 24 years before he retired at the rank of Lieutenant Colonel during a time the military terms their 'Don't Ask, Don't Tell' policy era. This 'Don't Ask, Don't Tell' policy has only recently been revoked by the armed services. He retired at the end of 1999. If he would have been exposed as being gay during his active duty years, he would most likely have been charged with Dereliction of Duty and probably would have been discharged.

I've talked with another retired officer who played racquetball with my ex, and I asked her, post-discovery, if she ever thought he was gay. She said, "Yes, when I first met him, but then I met you and your children, and so I no longer thought he might be gay." Wow – how *incredibly* convenient our children and I were for him! She also added that after his USAF retirement when he was working for a government contract company, it was known that he had been verbally abusive to clients. This did not surprise me.

Yet I've often wondered why I have been so overwhelmed with such a feeling of emptiness after my gay husband left me. Why wasn't I leaping for joy that this verbal and emotional abuser was gone?

As of this writing it has been over four years since he left, but I am still in recovery. In my quiet moments, on a daily basis, I still cannot believe it all. The emptiness comes from the loneliness I feel now at the absence of what "should have been." I had invested so much in *our* life together, and now it was all lost – gone forever. All I ever wanted was to be close to him, to laugh and talk, watch movies together – just normal everyday stuff would have made me happy. But he was gone most of the time on so-called business trips, network marketing meetings, hot air ballooning, and whatever distraction that he could invent in order to spend as much time away from home as possible.

I had been deceived by him for so many years. This realization, once discovery occurred, literally took my breath away as the trauma took hold. I believed in him completely, and yet I was the fool who had been fooled. My world no longer felt safe. The person whom I trusted the most became the person who personified evil to me. I felt afraid of him. At first I was numb. I didn't know what I was supposed to think or feel or say. The depth of my despair surprised me. I thought of him as a demon, and his Halloween costume was designed to make him look like an honorable, respectful, honest, man. For so many years his Air Force uniform seemed to clothe him with integrity. Now I could no longer bear to gaze at him. I hoped that he would never again violate my world.

When he left, I began to lose my identity because my sense of "self" was tied to him, and I realized that I was experiencing *"depersonalization disorder" (when there exists a loss of contact with your own personal reality accompanied by feelings of unreality and strangeness)*. This was "the fog" that many straight wives experience – when we finally realize that our entire marriage wasn't real – it was all crazy! Only *after* "discovery" can we begin the stages of finally realizing that our gut was right all along! Add this incredible realization with the loss of a "loved one," for the person who we thought we loved has now been forever lost. Soon after he left is when I discovered he was gay. And I think, "Where did my husband go?" on so many levels.

In times of trouble, many look to God. I was afraid that I would lose faith, as many have, when bad things happen. I had many conversations with God. I asked him why he made some people gay. No answer. Through my childhood education, I learned in Catholic school that marriage is a sacrament – that vows are promises to God. I learned that "for richer or poorer, in sickness and in health … 'til death us do part." I kept my part of the deal. I stayed with this man, knowing that he wasn't quite right, always in hopes that he would one day get some counseling help. Did my God abandon me? I was faithful to my husband, trusted him, and God made him gay. The bible said, "But in the beginning God made a man and a woman. That's why a man leaves his father and mother and gets married" Mark 10.6-7. Nowhere did it say that some men shall be homosexual and trick the woman into marriage.

Did God trick me too? How does God fit into my life now? I knew He wasn't going to make my life easy. He's already taken my mom, dad, sister, aunts and uncles, and now my husband, not through death of my ex, although it would have been easier, I think, if he would have died. Death has reasons. Gay didn't make any sense.

And now, all that's left is me.

Most women will never know the truth because very few gay married men will ever admit it. Most people think, "Come on, why didn't you know?" For most people outside of this relation-ship, it is very hard to understand how otherwise intelligent women could be so deceived. When living within this relation-ship, you accept the status-quo without question. Many women who have a gay husband simply do not know what he is doing every second of every day. These are the ones who say, "My husband gets up in the morning, goes to work and comes home at the usual hour, and remains home." Little do these women know that these men use the Internet to hook up with other men for a "quickie" in restrooms at a restaurant, train stations, cruise ships, Home Depot, Walmart, airports, and anywhere else you can think of. Heck – these women are, often times in the same restaurant with their husbands while they excuse themselves for a few minutes to go to the restroom to have anonymous sex. Any public restroom will do for a quick encounter.

Living within this "marriage," I asked myself constantly, "Why doesn't he treat me with kindness and respect? What's wrong with me?" He made me internalize blame for everything – why I couldn't shop right – why I couldn't do the laundry right – why I couldn't do this or that right. After my daughter was born I had gained weight (I had post-partum depression and an undiag-nosed thyroid condition). Now I was disgusting as well. He never introduced me as his "wife." In fact, around the house, he never even used my name.

Truly, most of my trauma stems from so many years I worked on our relationship and how he watched me trying everything to make him happy. No matter how hard I tried, it was never enough. This was truly abusive. I value truth so very much, and it pains me deeply to know that I spent so many years of my life with a liar.

I look back over 27 years of marriage (30 years when the divorce was finalized) and realize that I was depressed much of the time and constantly wondered why our marriage didn't make sense – why he was constantly gone, why I wasn't allowed an opinion regarding our finances, why he spent so much money, why he verbally abused me, why he was so quick to anger over trivial things and why there was no intimacy, no relationship, no respect – because he forbade it, and I accepted it as it was, always hoping that he would agree to go to counseling with me, and he would one day be "fixed."

I kept thinking that if I tried harder, he would "get better." I didn't really think that I was being abused since he never struck me. I truly believed whatever he said and blamed me for was accurate. I think back now and find it all hard to believe. When it's happening to you, you fall for it somehow.

I was the submissive, troubled wife. I learned to be submissive to keep the peace in the marriage. Troubled, because in my gut, I knew there was something wrong. Before I discovered he was gay, I knew that he was a dictator and a narcissist, for only HIS way and what HE wanted was my only reality. After time, I learned quite well that my opinion was not his concern. This domination almost gave me a direction and purpose in life – to try at all times to please my "husband." I just came to accept the fact that what he said mattered, and whatever I thought or said, didn't. I would just shake my head and not utter a word, for I knew it was futile to confront him.

He frequently had hissy-fits and temper tantrums over trivial things, but his anger was always directed at me. He always avoided conflicts and refused to communicate. He simply clammed up and refused to talk. I could never understand why he wouldn't or couldn't communicate with me.

In the early stages of our relationship, we enjoyed each other's company, but it was absent of the playful and affectionate behavior that I saw in other couples. Our relationship was never like that. I didn't question his behavior as I had begun to have deep feelings for him. I just accepted his individuality.

Time passed and we grew closer, but there was still some kind of "front" that he had about him. His personality wasn't fun-loving – a little bit mechanical, or what I thought was intellectual. He had a B.S. in Chemistry after all, and so I thought that was why. He was just really smart, which he was, and that impressed me a great deal.

Thinking back on many events of my life, after gay disclosure, I can't help but wonder about a lot of events being not what they seemed at the time. But with gay enlightenment now, things make much more sense. Epiphanies, if you will. I've thought back to the beginning of my relationship with him and have analyzed a great deal of past events and conversations. The first of these was when we were dating in 1977, and Lawrence was at my parents' house. My Dad walked in, and announced that he had just paid off the house in full. *Now* I think, "Did Lawrence take a mental note of this?" He told my Dad, "I hope that I'll be able to do that one day."

Since I worked for Pan Am at that time, I was eligible for free travel. Lawrence liked the idea of flying commercial instead of on air force planes. He knew that if he married me that he, also, would be eligible for free travel – First Class too!

I fell in love with him during a 3-month absence of his when he went on an Air Force "TDY." We had been dating almost a year at this time. When he returned from this TDY, he asked me to marry him – kind of. I say kind of, because, he didn't really ASK. I saw on an Oprah show where Dina McGreevy was a guest, and she was talking about her new book. She was married to the N.J. Senator McGreevy who admitted he was gay, after he was blackmailed by his partner. Dina said the same thing that I had experienced, namely, he didn't really ASK her to marry him either.

Lawrence invited me to dinner at a Japanese restaurant in Seattle. After dinner, he got out the ring, and opened it before me, and said, just like Dina McGreevy said her husband proposed, was, "Here's this ring. What do you think?" I told him it's beautiful. He told me that I have become "very dear" to him, and that he cared for me deeply. I kept looking at the ring, and didn't say a lot - just did a lot of thinking. There's something missing here, I thought. I knew I should question him if he loved me, but I thought that I was probably okay with what he said. My gut-instinct told me that it still just didn't feel quite like it should.

Lawrence told me that he talked with some of his flying buddies in the Air Force (he was a C-130 Navigator, stationed at McChord AFB), and he told them that he wasn't sure if I'd accept his marriage proposal. They asked him why. He said, "I don't know." Looking back, it was probably because of the "love" thing. He couldn't bring himself to tell me that he *loved* me, and he was wondering himself, if "I care for you deeply" would cut it. I just thought he was shy.

So we got married. For our honeymoon, Lawrence wanted me to get free First-Class tickets to Europe, through my job. I kind of wanted to go on a romantic honeymoon, to Hawaii, but since we had the opportunity to go to Europe, First Class, that was fine with me.

At first everything was good in our marriage, but then he started getting in little digs at me. First, he called me stupid when I went to the store and didn't get the right thing that he asked for. I bought a prepared pound-cake for his strawberries instead of those individual mini-cakes. Next he told me how *beautiful* his sister looked on her wedding day. I told him that he never commented on how *I* looked on our wedding day, even though I told him how great he looked. Then he said, "You looked *nice*." Then there was, "There isn't anything I wouldn't do for my sister." More and more he was throwing me off-guard every chance he got--making me "second-guess" much of what he said. There seemed to be a lack of free-flowing communication. So I'm thinking, "Well, he married me, so I am assuming that he would feel the same way about me, right?"

Yet, I never heard an "I love you" from him. I began to feel that he didn't love me because his actions spoke for him. He began to be critical, pontificating, patriarchic, and I began to experience a sense of uneasiness in his presence as he began to direct his occasional anger toward me–not the nurturing, embracing, accepting kind of person that I would expect from someone who I married.

I noticed that he stopped wearing his wedding ring a couple of months after we were married. I asked him why and he said that it's just easier to leave it off because since he's not allowed to wear jewelry of any kind when he flies, that it's just easier to not wear anything so he doesn't have to remember to put it on or take it off. (Flight crews were not allowed to wear jewelry when flying)

He got orders for Rhein Main Airbase, Frankfurt, Germany, so we moved there in 1982. For two years we had a great time going on volksmarches (5 km hikes in the woods, usually sponsored by a city or town) and traveling within the country, going to many castles. We also had a couple of trips outside of Germany, to Holland and Italy. His attitude was pretty good there. We had some good times, and things were okay.

He admitted to me that occasionally he'd go out to xxx-rated movies in Frankfurt. I told him that I didn't want him to do that anymore. I thought he stopped because he said he would. But once while he was TDY, I got a call in the middle of the night from two giggling German women asking for him by name. I questioned him, and of course, it must have been a wrong number.

One day in 1982, he came home and just announced as he was walking down the hallway that he thinks it's time that I get pregnant. He didn't even look at me. Again, I thought, "Wow, this is strange. What a way to say to your wife that you would like a child." I didn't say anything to him about that, but I should have, in hindsight. At the time, I just brushed it all aside, again, in my attempt to protect my psyche. It took us a while to get pregnant because he wore briefs instead of boxers. I told him then and before that I loved him, to which he replied, "Uh huh."

Our daughter was born in December of 1984. Soon after, we moved to North Carolina for Lawrence's new assignment at Pope Air Force Base, in North Carolina, as a C-130 Instructor Navigator.

Lawrence bought a new house in Fayetteville, NC. I wanted a single-story house, since having the baby, it would have been easier than a two-story, but he bought a two-story. I couldn't complain. It was a really nice, brand new house. I thought it was a little too expensive for us, but I was just becoming aware that he really didn't listen very much to what I said or wanted.

Lawrence didn't seem to have much of an interest in Annie. He had many TDY's (Air Force jargon, for business trips) and was gone a LOT. When he was home, he wasn't much help with Annie. If she cried at night, he would never get up unless she was throwing up in her crib. Only then would he get up and hold her while I changed her sheets. I didn't understand his lack of understanding as I was dealing with sleep deprivation, post partum depression, and an undiagnosed thyroid problem, which made me all the more exhausted. He had absolutely no empathy. When he was home, he was becoming more and more disconnected. He busied himself with chores outside in the yard, mostly at times I needed him, like when I was preparing dinner, and the baby needed attention.

I felt like he gave the orders, and I had to obey him, as if I were a child. I realized he was narcissistic, and he made me very unhappy. He never joked. Everything was serious with him. He had frequent "hissy-fits" and temper tantrums. I resigned myself to life without love and affection because that was my reality.

After Annie was a year old, my Mom was diagnosed with a liver tumor. She went to live with my sister, near Chicago, who was able to care for her. My sister called me just before Annie was two and told me that I should get ready to go, because my Mom was near death. Lawrence was on TDY when I got this call from my sister. I was obviously upset, so I called his superior officer and told him that I needed to speak with Lawrence in order to make arrangements for me to go. I was clearing my head and thinking of house, dog, baby, transportation, and what to do about each. Lawrence got on the phone, and I told him that my Mom was dying and he said, "So what do you want me to do about it?" My heart, it seemed, dropped to my feet in disbelief of what I just heard. I don't know why I didn't just hang up on him. I guess the only reason was I needed answers to many questions. It was like being pierced in the heart with a knife. It was devastating. Not only did I have to deal with the news about my mom, but in addition, I felt this horrible apathy from my husband! He never apologized.

It was only six weeks later, after my mom passed away, that I got another call from my sister that my father was in intensive care. Lawrence told me I couldn't go, that we couldn't afford it because of the house payment. This house that I knew was too expensive for our budget, remember? My sister, Bonnie, said she would pay for my ticket. Lawrence said I could go then, but only according to his schedule – Annie's second birthday was the following week, and he said that I had to wait for that before he'd *allow* me to go. By the time I saw my Dad, he wasn't able to talk any more. I'm sure he was laying in intensive care, wondering why I wasn't there. I wondered, "Who did I marry? Why is he so arrogant?" I attended my father's funeral alone with Annie and other family members.

In 1987 we moved to Wright-Patterson AFB, Ohio, and we lived on the airbase in housing quarters. Annie loved her pre-school there and life was okay there. Lawrence occasionally had hissy-fits and tantrums, but I knew he had a temper. His Dad had a temper, and I understood that he learned this from his father. I didn't know his father, but already I didn't like him. I hoped he would get better so Annie didn't learn it too. On this one occasion, my friend came over and asked if I would watch her two children while she took her oldest child to the doctor. Her oldest daughter had just broken her leg at school. I said I would, and in my friend's presence, Lawrence said, "I have plans," in a clearly perturbed manner. My friend quietly said, "It's okay, I'll find someone else." My friend and I looked at each other with our mouths open. Lawrence's only plans were to go out to dinner that evening – nothing important.

In 1989, Lawrence was gone for one year on a "remote" tour of duty to Diego Garcia (in the middle of the Indian Ocean). He was stationed at Kirtland Air Force Base then, in Albuquerque, NM. Annie was five then, and we kept each other company that year. He was able to return home at the six-month point of his tour of duty for a two week visit. If I didn't know better, it seemed like he was trying to get me pregnant. This time there was no announcement of his intentions or any talk about the possibility of pregnancy. I did, however, get pregnant. When he returned home after that year, he was in the best mood I have ever witnessed in him. He was happy to be home, and it showed. He was affectionate and a pleasure to be around – for a while.

On this one day, while I was in my 8th month, I was cleaning the closet and found condoms in Lawrence's jacket pocket. I confronted him, and he told me that he had been to some rated xxx-rated movies and jacked himself off. He used the condoms to catch the mess. Gay didn't even enter my mind. Yes, admittedly, I was naïve, but I thought our marriage was based on truth, so I believed him. I do remember one thing he said at the time, and for some reason, it stuck in my head, after all these years. During our conversation, he said, "It just feels so natural." I thought then, "Hmm – what feels so natural – mastur-bating?" It just seemed odd.

After our son was born, all sexual relations ended – just all of a sudden. Nothing was spoken, but I knew. It was during this time that he bought a hot air balloon and went to South Dakota for 2 weeks for instruction to fly it. I stayed home with Annie and baby Marc and was experiencing post partum depression and sleep deprivation again. I remember praying to God to just take my miserable life from me. At that time, I didn't even know I could have asked for medicine at least for the post partum depression. I wasn't told, so I did the best that I could. Again, another time that I needed my husband the most, he disap-pointed me again. All I wanted was some sleep, and he left to go ballooning for 2 weeks. I didn't know what a mental "breakdown" was exactly, but I thought I was having one. I remember nursing Marc in the wee hours in the living room, crying from exhaustion and having the thought of wanting to take a baseball bat and hit all of the ornaments on the Christmas tree. I knew it was crazy. Why would I think such a thing? Was I having some type of breakdown?

Hot-air ballooning was Lawrence's passion every weekend. He got up early, usually 4 a.m., which always woke me up, and he came back late in the afternoon and took a nap. I would have liked a nap myself since I didn't get very much sleep, nursing Marc frequently throughout the night. But I knew not to expect any compassion from him – or help.

Every Saturday, while Lawrence was out ballooning, I took Annie to the skating rink with Marc in his stroller. This was very difficult, as Marc wanted to get out of his stroller, yet I couldn't allow it because of the danger of people on skates zooming everywhere. Lawrence also began "network marketing" in Amway. This is a company based on the premise of "the pyramid," where you "get" someone into the "business," and then your pyramid builds, with promises of untold wealth. I thought it was a load of crap, but this company and ballooning became his new wife and family. The kids and I were mere ornaments for the house. I felt like I was expected to walk on eggshells when he was on the phone, trying to convince people to join his pyramid scheme, which never happened. Well, he actually got one guy in. He yelled at me for not keeping the kids quiet while he was on the phone. I realized that everything ELSE was more important to him than his family. I knew we weren't worth his time. Only HE mattered – no empathy – only abandonment.

I remember one day, going through our storage stuff, and I came upon my wedding dress. In tears, I brought it upstairs, to donate it to charity. My deceased mom made that dress for me. I couldn't stand to see it any more. I realized that I didn't have a happy marriage. I didn't know what was wrong.

This same year, Lawrence announced that he had to move to Saudi Arabia. He told me that I could stay in our house in Albuquerque with the kids if I wanted, but he'd be gone for a couple of years. What kind of a husband and father is that? I told him that if I stayed behind with the kids, that that would not be a good thing for our family. I also thought that's strange for him to leave Albuquerque at a time when he knew he would be a top-contender for making the rank of full colonel because he worked with a general who Lawrence thought surely would and could promote him. Why? I didn't know. I knew that this was NOT a mandatory move, but we all moved to Saudi, and when the review board met while we were there, Lawrence did NOT make full colonel. The two-star general in Saudi was unable to grant him the promotion.

While living in Saudi, Joyce, the colonel's wife, visited us one day by herself. She was the full colonel's wife, whose husband was Lawrence's boss. Joyce asked me for a sandwich since the compound's restaurant was closed. Lawrence walked into the kitchen some time later and asked me if I had gotten her something to eat in a manner in which Joyce took note of. She said his tone was on the mean side. She noticed it, and remembered it.

There is one thing in particular that I remembered while living in Saudi. Lawrence commented to me that when a Saudi man wants to divorce his wife, all that is necessary is for him to say, "I divorce you," and it's a done deal – no lawyers or anything. He must have been very envious. At the time, I just thought it was an interesting tid-bit of Saudi culture.

I now think back when I was studying Psychology in college, and not understanding this phenomenon, called Stockholm Syndrome. I thought I was smarter than that! At the time I was in college, I thought these women who take verbal and/or physical abuse from their 'significant others' are just stupid. It didn't make sense that ANYONE would allow that to happen to them and then, many even made excuses for their 'significant other.' Little did I know at that time that Stockholm Syndrome would be in MY future! These master manipulators have the ability to somehow convince you that your life with them is normal.

In 1995, after living only one year in Saudi, the kids and I were evacuated after two bombs exploded, one bomb, killing 19 service men and women. We moved to an apartment in Las Vegas to be near Lawrence's brother and his family for one year while Lawrence remained in Saudi finishing his duty tour. Then we could rejoin him in our Albuquerque home. After that year was over, we moved back into our home in Albuquerque, NM for the next several years.

In November 1999, Lawrence retired from the USAF. He served for almost 24 years. The Air Force gave me some "thank you" mementos at his retirement ceremony. It was customary for the husband to acknowledge his wife's contribution during this ceremony, but I didn't expect or receive any words of appreciation from him, even though I am sure, most of the room, expected to hear something regarding that.

Some time later, Lawrence's mom was visiting us. We were all going to Colorado. Lawrence asked me to get gas while he was at work so we wouldn't have to stop later. I was busy getting stuff together while visiting with his Mom, and time had gotten away from me. *I forgot to get gas!* Lawrence came home and asked if I had gotten gas. When Lawrence found out that I forgot, he verbally assaulted me in front of his Mom. All she said to him was, "You need to calm down before you have a heart attack." How crazy is that?

Thinking back, I don't know why I didn't go over and slap him across the face! I remember thinking about wanting to do that. I thought his mother's words were insane! I thought to myself, "Who gives a CRAP about him? He is verbally assaulting me because I forgot to get gas, and you're worried HE might have a heart attack because he was having a hissy-fit?" How CRAZY is that?

Who was it that was yelling at me? Well, it sure wasn't the man who loved me. That man wouldn't do that kind of thing. He had disappeared a long time ago, when I wasn't looking, and now I was looking at a stranger. And all that time I'd been thinking he was the man I'd married.

If the cupboards in the kitchen were open, he slammed them closed. If the dishwasher was left open, he slammed it closed. I didn't understand his anger. Why was he walking around with so much anger? Was it my fault? What did I do? So many,

many, "little things," that made me feel horrible inside, from the slamming of drawers to looking for an item that he felt sure that I had moved around and couldn't find. He even blamed me because Marc couldn't play basketball very well. He said that I let him play too many video games instead of making him practice basketball. Lawrence bought Marc a basketball hoop but never played with him – so it's my fault that Marc couldn't play basketball because I didn't make him practice? I could never do anything right, or could never, ever, measure up to what I should be for him. The criticism was constant. I would drive everywhere because he wanted to talk on his cell phone, yet he'd never tell me who he was talking to – only "a friend."

Then Lawrence announced yet again, that we were to move-this time to California. We lived there for a couple of years, and then Lawrence wanted to move yet again to Washington State. He told me that if we bought a place in Washington, then he could commute to Las Vegas or *wherever his company needed him*, and that way we would have a stable residence for our kids and a place that we could retire later. It all made sense at the time, sort of, I guess, even though I didn't like it and sensed that there was still something wrong with all of this. I still didn't buy his angle. I was confused.

With gay enlightenment now, I can see that Lawrence kept us on the move so much because he was afraid of being discovered and was probably concerned that I would make friends and confidants who could help me decipher the abuse in it all. Abusers like to isolate their victims.

Our first spring on the farm, Lawrence planted over 400 blueberry bushes. He used the farm as a tax shelter. Sometime later we took Marc to a University of Washington tennis outing. I was listening to music on my iPod and spoke a little loudly. I didn't listen often and forgot that you tend to speak more loudly when you have music playing in your ears. Lawrence mockingly laughed hysterically at me because he said I had Alzheimer's, which was a frequent "name" he called me when he wanted to get his jollies at my expense. I often wondered why he didn't laugh like that WITH me instead of AT me.

The farm was just another way to use me. I could protect his tax shelter (the farm) during the week. He expected me to hand-water all 400 blueberry bushes. All the while he was living in Las Vegas, making many side-trips to Albuquerque, where his boyfriend, Steve lived, doing whatever he wanted to do during the week, with no accountability.

But everything began going to pieces the summer of 2006 when we went to Hawaii. He dumped our daughter, son, and me off at one beach while he went to a nude beach. Post gay discovery, I 'Googled' Little Beach, Maui and found it to be a gay nude beach. He came back to pick us up 4 hours later, when it was dark.

In the beginning of October 2006, he wrote a note to me and left it on my computer keyboard:

"I am sorry we can't talk. I am sorry we have no "empathy" to facilitate talking. I am sorry we don't get along. I am sorry I am so mixed up. I am sorry I am having problems. I am sorry those problems affect so many other things. I am sorry those things affect me the way they do and I am having so many challenges dealing with them. I am sorry."

So WHAT, exactly, is he apologizing to me for? Again, I was confused. He's apologizing to me because he's having problems? At first I thought about asking him why he's so mixed up and wanting to help him with whatever problems he was having. Yet somehow, it still didn't sound like a sincere apology to me. If someone says they're sorry, it is usually because they want to make amends to the person they hurt. This wasn't that. Since he has NEVER apologized to me for ANYTHING, I knew all of the "I am sorry's" were all lies. He has NEVER told me he was sorry for all of the verbal and emotional abuse that I have endured from him, so why should he be sorry now? He said, "I am sorry we can't talk." All of these years I wondered why he wasn't able to communicate! It was all so twisted!

Then I found an enlightening article about spotting emotional manipulation. The article explained that emotional manipulation is also covert aggression. There were some interesting points made in this article. One that stood out in my mind was the saying of the word "Sorry." Even as you hear the word, you get the sensation that they really do NOT mean they are sorry at all. But since they've said the word, you're pretty much left with nothing more to say. Either that or you suddenly find yourself babysitting *their* angst!! Under all circumstances if you feel this angle is being played, don't capitulate! Do not accept an apology that feels like it is phony. Rule number one - if dealing with an emotional blackmailer, TRUST your gut. TRUST your senses. Once an emotional manipulator finds a successful maneuver, it's added to his repertoire, and you'll be fed a steady diet of this."

The article went on to explain that when an emotional manipulator is sad or angry, it brings a deep instinctual response to find some way to equalize the emotional climate. What we end up doing is making the emotional manipulator feel better by trying to fix whatever is broken for him. The words that really hit me were, "Stick with this type of loser for too long and you will be so enmeshed and co-dependent you will forget you even have needs - let alone that you have just as much right to have your needs met." Wow, wow, wow!

I then knew that I was correct in trusting my gut and not allowing myself to be taken in by his craziness. I answered his "I am sorry's" with a written account of his verbal and emotional abuses over the years and emailed it to him. My gut feeling about him was right-on!

Why was he angry with me because I had enough of his verbal and emotional abuse? Shouldn't he realize how much he has hurt me and want to stop? That's what a normal person would think, but I have learned so very much since then.

He told me that he didn't love me and *never did*, and he *didn't have empathy and didn't know where to get it.* I wonder if he was conscious of the fact that he just described himself as a psychopath.

A psychopath exhibits some or all of these behaviors:

Self-centeredness, lack of guilt, lack of moral sense, inability to control impulses, inability to form meaningful relationships, *deliberately deceives and shows no remorse, always feels like the victim, believes they don't do anything wrong. Wow!*

He continued. He said that we have "grown apart," and I should find someone else, and "*We were never meant to be together.*" I didn't know at the time, but I know and understand his meaning now! Now I understand why we were never meant to be together. Now I know that he is a coward and an evil-doer for not telling me WHY we were never meant to be together. Only he knew why, and he made ME internalize the blame for the failure of our marriage.

He told me many times over that, "There's no one else." His repetition of those words I thought sounded suspicious, and it seemed obvious that since he was over-emphasizing this point that just the opposite was REALLY true.

He also said, "The things you say – I don't care." That's why I thought he was going stupid because no matter what I said to him, he didn't listen or care. I asked him why he asked me to marry him. He said, "I don't know." He knew, but refused to tell me that I was merely used as his cover and breeder.

I asked him if he was gay at the request of two of my friends, and he chuckled and said, "<u>*Huh, No*</u>!" They both suspected this. I thought they were off the mark. When he told me he didn't love me, it felt so horrible. He said it so bluntly, it was obvious that he wanted to hurt me. So, after over 27 years of marriage, he was never able to say, "I love you," yet with casual ease, was able to tell me he didn't love me and never did. He wanted to just throw me away because he thought I was becoming too much of a risk of having a heart attack, stroke, cancer, or some other disease. That's what happened to a guy at work! He said that now this guy has to take care of his wife!

So to Lawrence, my only use was my role as a nanny, cook, maid, errand girl, and more recently, farm hand. That's all I was. That's all I was worth to him. That was a very painful reality. I was robbed of respect and was only used and abused for so many years. I put SO MUCH effort into trying to make my marriage work, and he didn't have the decency to tell me that all my efforts were in vain. *My heart ached for ME – for my raped spirit.* I was constantly crying. I couldn't stop.

Surely he must be having an affair. So I requested the last three months of cell phone statements in paper form to be mailed to me. Sure enough there was one phone number that stood out. I called it, and there was a recording on the other end, and he said, "Hi. This is Steven. Leave a message." I actually put the statements away for about a month, thinking Steve is just some guy he works with. But I made a table of all the calls to/from Steve – the date, hour, and duration of the call and emailed it to friends and family asking what they thought. My brother replied, "How could it be anything else?" I was truly blind-sided that his affair was with another man!

I confronted him. I asked him how long he and Steve had been a number. I was so nervous, my knees were shaking. I also asked, "How many Steves have there been?" He said, in total calmness, "*None of your business.*" Looking at him, all I could think was, "Where did my husband go? You never were my husband, were you?" I was so confused. I tried to make sense of my 27 years with him. I said, "So you just used me as your cover and a breeder for your children just to protect your Air Force career?" My reality for the last 27 years of my life was all an illusion.

So he thinks it's *none of my business*? I entered into a kind of reality warp – another dimension, it seemed. I couldn't think or concentrate. He said something about the checkbooks and that I could have some money, but I wasn't able to hear all of his words. For weeks I sat in my rocking chair, huddled in my fuzzy bathrobe, trying to follow whatever storyline that was on TV, but at the end of the show, I was lucky to know the name of the show or movie that I was watching. I started going to senior exercise classes at the gym. On this one occasion, tears would be flowing as I was exercising, and the instructor in the middle of exercises stopped and came over and gave me a hug.

Lawrence had always told me for years that occasionally I might get a call from Secretive Investigative Services since he had a Top Secret government clearance. They had called me several times since we moved to Chehalis, WA in 2004, with just some general questions – nothing that would raise alarm – I just thought they were updating their records. But I also got phone calls from a few other people, telling me that Secret Investigative Services had called them, as well.

My friend, Joyce (who the reader remembers that I met while in Saudi Arabia), told me that normally the Feds NEVER call the wife – NEVER! She asked Generals' wives if they ever get called. ALL of them said, "Never."

Secret Investigative Services OPM called me again soon after Lawrence asked me for a divorce and asked whose idea it was to divorce. I told them that it was his idea; however, I recently found out that he's a homosexual. They were unaware of this news. They told me that they were concerned that a closeted gay might be in a position of blackmail, and that's not good since he held such a high-level clearance.

As a result of the Feds knowing Lawrence's secret, they gave him an ultimatum. If he wanted to keep his government clearance and his job, then he would have to step out of his closet and tell all the people he knew. And so he did.

For Christmas, 2006, Lawrence was going to drive my son and me to the airport and stay at the house to watch our two dogs during our absence. After he arrived, I walked up to him and asked, "Why are you doing this?" "Doing what?" I thought, how incredibly stupid he is! "Leaving me for a guy?" I didn't understand – I thought his being gay was a choice. I didn't understand anything then. I didn't even know then that he was gay long before the day we first met.

All I wanted and needed was his truthfulness – but he didn't have the character and integrity for that. Instead, he said, "Don't do this." Why can't I expect a truthful response from him? All I heard were lies for our entire married life. Didn't he even have the decency to treat me like a real person and give me an honest answer?

I asked again why he's leaving me for a guy. I heard the same response, "Don't do this." I was getting so incredibly mad by this point. I stood in front of him as he tried to ignore me and walk past me. I blocked his movement again and demanded an answer. I really wanted to know why he thought it was okay to play with my life. He moved past me and walked out. I pushed him as he walked out the door from behind. He didn't fall. He wasn't hurt. I could have pushed him A LOT harder. He deserved to be shot! When I tell friends what happened, most respond, "You mean that's ALL you did?" What an incredible piece of work he is! The man has no decency at all.

What right did this person have to VIOLATE me AND allow trash to come into my home--and probably into my bed--to live a lie and deceive? He had NO right to do that. He had NO right to USE me. All of those incidences of emotional and verbal abuses flooded me moments before I pushed him.

I knew that I could not think in a rational manner at this point, as I thought about my Dad in intensive care and my not being able to go to him right away--the times that I needed him the most when I was sleep deprived when both of my children were babies – all the hissy-fits over such trivial things that made me feel awful – it all came to me as if I were dying, and my life was flashing before me. I kept thinking, "And I put up with you, ignoring my own happiness and desires for almost 30 years for what? So I could be your cover?"

In the end I received not even a simple explanation, no heart-to-heart exchange about his struggle or my role in his life over the past 28 years, absolutely nothing. Why did I try so hard trying to keep our marriage together for so, so, long? He watched all of my efforts, and only he knew it would never work.

This is what made me absolutely furious. He played with my life. I would have NEVER married him if I knew the secret he was hiding. What a fraud! How abusive!

After I pushed him, he walked over and stood in front of his truck, a dozen or so yards away. He looked at me for quite a while, probably in disbelief that I actually pushed him. For a moment we just stared at each other. Then I said, "YOU BASTARD!" He got in his truck and sped away.

He called the sheriff on me! He didn't allow me to be upset? I'm not even entitled to that after finding out that I have been so deceived for so many years and he called the sheriff on me? He thinks that I'm the bad person? He has destroyed me AND our family, but I'm the bad guy?

Here's some stuff Lawrence wrote through his lawyer:

"I have *recently* admitted to myself and to my family that I am a gay man." (Ahh, he forgot to add, "After my wife found out") I then admitted it to my other family members." Translation: Actually, after my talk with the Secret Investigative Services, I had to come out of my closet or be denied my top secret clearance, which my job requires. In fact, he never *admitted* anything to me, our grown daughter, or our son except in this legal document he sent through his lawyer. I don't believe he would have EVER told me the truth on his own accord. I only see him as an abusive psychopathic, lying and deceiving coward. For when I first asked him if he was gay, the reader should recall his response was "Huh! No!"

Additionally, he wrote in this legal document, "This has been an incredibly difficult time for me, my wife, our son, and our extended family. I understand I have caused pain to my loved ones, but I could no longer continue *living the lie I had lived for so many years*." So he *recently* admitted to himself that he was living the lie for *so many years*. Is it just me, or is there a contradiction here? If you have sex with men, why does it take over three decades to admit you're gay? And he understands he has caused pain to his loved ones? Well, he obviously wasn't referring to me as a 'loved one,' nor did he care that he has caused me pain – in fact, he delighted in causing me pain.

So, "I have *recently* admitted to myself and to my family that I am a gay man." and "....*living the lie I had lived for so many years.*" I did not understand this contradiction. At the time I read that statement I didn't understand the most terrible truth about denial is that you don't even know you're mired in it because the self-deception is so complete. Up until that point, I surmised, he could not accept the identity that was his to claim: a gay man.

How I wish that I could explain it to him now - that it is sooo *'gay'* to think that you're NOT gay, when you sleep with men or solicit gay sex in a Home Depot restroom! We have a winner for the Crown of Denial!

An email from Marc to Lawrence: "And let me remind you that it's your fault for everything.

Lawrence's response to Marc: ..."And believe it or not it is not all my fault. Love Dad"

My married daughter, Annie, emailed me following a short visit with her father: "He still thinks himself the victim in all of this, which is just insane. I don't know how his mind came to that conclusion."

I think back over the years now, after Discovery, trying to make sense I was watching the Animal Planet TV show, one day and there was a chimp that had been caged and abused. The commentator said, "This animal has lost his spirit. How do you come back from the dead after you've lost your spirit?" I thought then, "I don't know." I hope that one day I will be able to reclaim that part of me that has been lost .of so many things that I simply shrugged away at the time. I thought he had a problem with hemorrhoids. He did, and now I know why! Over the years, I wondered why he always had such problems. He used to use TUX, but it didn't help him very much. With both of my pregnancies I had hemorrhoid problems toward the end, and I found that Vitamin A & D ointment really helped, so I told him about it. He ALWAYS kept a tube of A &D on top of the toilet tank for as long as I can remember. So many 'light-bulb' moments came to mind! I never understood the enemas either. I found enemas in the bathroom cupboards. Post gay discovery, I learned that they like to clean themselves out before they have sex.

I talked with Lawrence's brother and he told me that Lawrence told him and his other family members and friends that he just turned gay *recently*. They believed him.

On Oprah Winfrey's show, which aired 8 February 2010, she was speaking with child molesters. She asked one of the molesters, "What do you think you did to her?" He answered, "I killed who she could have been. Basically, I murdered a person and just because she's still alive today and walking around and breathing and getting her life back on-track, that doesn't take away from anything that I've done."

Oprah said, "That is one of the most powerful things that I have ever heard anyone say - (I killed who she could have been) - because that is the absolute truth - when a child (or anyone for that matter), is abused, it changes who they are – it kills their spirit." At least this child molester had a conscience and was able to see the harm he has done.

I watch Criminal Minds a lot on TV. There was an episode where an abused wife shot her husband while he was in bed asleep. The teenaged children loathed their mom and told the investigators that their mom was a terrible mom, because she couldn't do anything right - couldn't shop and get the right stuff, couldn't do the laundry right, etc. They told the investigators that their mom was stupid. The investigators said, "So she was mentally challenged?" The siblings said, "No, just stupid." The investigators asked, "Who told you she was stupid?" They answered that their father said it all the time. Powerful stuff.

Thinking back I enjoyed being around him many years ago before he turned into a mean and angry person whom I began to barely tolerate. He had no time for our children and our family. He became only a source of security to me.

In the beginning of our relationship he made me feel like I had something to offer. I just never had a chance to offer it to someone better than him. I have forgiven myself for not leaving him so many years ago when it was obvious that the only thing that mattered to him was himself and his money. I knew long ago he never cared about Annie and Marc or me by his disconnected narcissistic air. In my own self-evaluation, I believe that I simply gave up and didn't care anymore. I was afraid of leaving him because I knew I would not be able to make a decent living on my own, and I didn't want my children to go through a divorce. I would have no emotional support, as I had no family or friends left. I had no "home" since we moved so frequently, people would ask where I'm from. I tell them that I'm not from anywhere. I was afraid of the unknown, so I accepted the fact that I could only watch as I saw other couples laugh with each other and hold hands.

Even though my gut always told me that there was something wrong with him, still I kept hoping that he would "get it" at some point. By his own admission, he lacked empathy, for without a conscience, the only thing that matters is 'Don't get caught' which was his only goal while in the Air Force.

My heart is broken. I remember when my heart used to feel joy, and I don't know if I will be able to get back there again. It was all too much for too long, with so many disappointments and broken dreams, all piled up on shattered trust. My naïveté scares me. How will I be able to trust anyone again?

Elaine's Story

In the autumn of 1986, I, an ordinary happy-go-lucky, fun-loving girl with a strong sense of adventure, returned to my home town, Grays, a little town in the county of Essex, England. I had just spent six months working in the Swiss Alps. While there, I was already saving and planning my next trip, a one year working holiday to Australia. My job as a chef allowed me to combine both career and travel. Life was good, and I was very happy.

The same winter, I decided to stay where I was for a few months longer in order to save the outstanding money to fund the trip. I was employed as pastry-chef at a reputed London Hotel, a stone's throw away from Buckingham Palace. There I met a very sweet French guy named Francois who was on a working holiday for one year in England.

There was something about him that appealed to me and made him stand apart from the other guys I had met. He was charismatic, polite, a gentleman, and took pride in his appearance. His sensibility reflected mine, and it before long, we became friends and began to see each other outside of work. I later learned that he was very close to his family. They had visited him twice during the year he was away, and he was going back to be with them for Christmas.

We both had a few gay friends/colleagues, but that was common in hotel and catering industry. I liked the fact that he was not homophobic and comfortable around gay men. This appealed to my own open-mined values of acceptance and tolerance of others regardless of their differences. I also concluded he must be okay with his own sexuality if he is so comfortable around gay men! We even went to gay drag-bars with colleagues (straight and gay), and he was very much at home there; in fact, he asked to go back there another time!

Our friendship blossomed, and it was not long before we become lovers. He was very demonstrative with his feelings and had no problem with public displays of affection towards me. He showered me with gifts. Everyone who met him fell for his charisma and charm, and it was not long before he was also winning the hearts of my entourage as I became the envy of all!

At one point it did cross my mind he may be gay. His room was far tidier than any other single guy's I had met before. He even had pop star posters of men on his walls, but I fobbed the idea off telling myself that he was French, and French guys were different than British guys. They were somehow more refined. I thought he was merely more in touch with his feminine side than the average bloke! Also he was dating me, so he couldn't possibly be gay, I thought!

After Christmas I decided not to travel to Australia alone, so he was happy to join me. I was thrilled with this idea, as was he, likewise. I started to realize that gay men were noticing him, but I figured he was a nice looking guy, so that was normal. During the flight to Australia, there was a gay guy in our aisle, and I think he would have made a pass at him if I had not been sitting between them! We both laughed it off and continued our trip. Sometimes our communication was a little stunted, but I put this down to the fact that he was Francophone and me Anglophone; however, both were keen to learn each other's language and culture which was another plus in my books! I figured with time when our vocabularies expanded, the connection would become richer and deeper too. We were both very much in love, and I was amazed how different we were culturally. And yet, we shared the same values and interests. I concluded that love did not come in a form of culture or language…it had a language all of its own, "the language of the heart!"

Our love life was one of passion, and we could not get enough of each other, discovering each other's minds and bodies like any other new couple in love. Six months later he went back to France, and I spent the next six challenging months on my own. The rupture was huge, and although I met many more people on my travels through and around Australia, my heart went with him. He was in my thoughts, and I could not get him out of my mind.

We wrote to each other every day until the year was up. Then I went back to Europe and we were reunited once again. I spent Christmas with my folks and was just itching to be back together with him. By New Year's, we reunited in Paris, drinking champagne and celebrating our togetherness while promising never to part! We were going to die together.

We lived in Paris for a while where I got to see him in his own culture, expressing himself in his own language ,in all his splendor, in this "Ville d'amour," rich in architectural beauty and culture.

We moved to the south of France soon after our stay in Paris. Country life suited us both better than city life. We married civilly in November of 1988. I was 23 years of age, and he was 24. He is Catholic, and I am Protestant; therefore, a church wedding would have proved complicated. A civil wedding with just close family members and friends was the best option. We honeymooned in Venice and were already planning to have a family together.

I come from a four-child family, a dysfunctional family with a loving but over-protective father with very deep seated control and violence issues and a loving but subservient mother who survived in fear but stayed in her marriage for the love of her children. Francois was from a three-child family, faux bourgeois family, which in its own way, was also dysfunctional. His mother was a kind but over-powering loving and very controlling, and his father was a cultured but hen-pecked man who worked away from home until he retired, bringing the bacon home, filling financial duties, but leaving emotional voids amongst his children.

We both wanted a 3-4 child family (at least) and hoped to fill it with the love we shared. We both planned to have a 'better' family we could call our own!

We started a family immediately after we were wed. Life was blissful. We were both following a dream and ideals...a family

was to be born.....our first child was born in 1989 just one day before New Year's Eve. Francois always struck me as a guy who loved kids, so I thought he would make the perfect father. I found it endearing to see him interact with other people's children. I could not wait to see him with our children!

We soon made a circle of friends, multi -cultural, gays and lesbians ...all men are equal--all were welcome. Francois was always the life and soul at the party; however, in our intimacy he was not a man of many words. He was kind of shy and introverted and never really willing to communicate on a deeper level. He was loving and caring, so I was okay with this. After all nobody is perfect, but given I was not one to believe in changing others, instead loving unconditionally, I found my equilibrium with motherhood and sought to fill voids by compensating with friendships out of the home. I figured he was this way because he was a guy, and I grew up with the belief that guys find it harder to express themselves when it came to their emotions. Therefore I had no real expectations. We were young when we met (I was 21 and he was 22) and consequently had limited experience with relationships and even less with marriage.

We grew closer to his parents who were now retired in the south of France, a stone's throw from us. They gave us the sense of belonging and security .it was a comfort to have them close by. In 1995, we became restless in France as the economic situation degraded considerably. We decided to live another adventure and looked into emigrating to Australia, South Africa, or Canada. Moving to Canada was the easier option as there were no occupation barriers or political problems there; on the contrary, they were seeking French speaking immigrants to boost the Francophone communities. So we sold our home and arrived in Quebec, with three young kids and three suitcases to our names.

We had the courage to start all over; our new life was here now in Canada. We made it our duty to stick together through thick and thin, and there was a strong sense of togetherness.

We were here miles from home in this together. We were going to make it work! That was our mantra!

We made new friends, got back into the workforce, and fast-forward a few years we were back on track. We replaced all the material stuff plus more. We added a few more kids, and we were now a happy and proud family living a busy but happy life with all the joys life has to offer. I even started work after taking ten years out to nurture our *brood* of then five!

It was good for me to get back into society and feel the self-worth of contributing physically and financially; however, because I was not the one pulling the family purse strings, unknown to me then, I was giving up my own financial independence in the bargain. I found myself fruitless and bootless, a volunteer on the home front. Everyone else's needs passed before my own. I was left with pangs of guilt if I dared to spend any of my hard earned money; however, the more money I earned, the more frivolous Francois became.

We had our ups and downs like every couple, but we pulled it together and things were always pretty smooth between us. We never argued and rarely fell out; if we did have disagreements, it was not long before we shook ourselves out of it and continued. We had both grown up with fights and bickering as part of daily life. And one thing was clear--neither wished for this in our own family. Rightly or wrongly, we both avoided conflict. I was often the one to back down and give in. Anything for a harmonious life.

In 2003, we had our sixth child, which kind of took everyone by surprise as our fifth child was already five at this time. The first batch of children was close in age. This time I was hospitalized as she was premature. This saga was quite the challenge for us all, but I had the strong conviction we could, with the strength and love of this big family, get through anything! While I was away, I was aware that I was missed by everyone, and my husband would divide his time between work, the kids, and visiting me. He could not wait for us to be back together again.

I felt that maybe he would finally realize all I did with raising the kids. Since I went back to work three years prior to this time, I found myself with less and less help on the home-front. I was expected to hold down the fort and work. I had two part-time jobs. I was starting to feel like a single parent as he had multiple career changes and jobs that took him away from home more and more. Still convinced we could get through any challenge in our path, I continued on the grounds that he was working hard for his family.

The years progressed, and I noticed we were forgetting ourselves as a couple. I seemed to be the only one who noticed and cared. When I suggested we re-ignite the flame, he would say, "Yes, good idea," but do nothing about it. He started to go to the gym, and when I suggested we do this as a couple like before, he would say it was not a good idea as we had nobody to care for the kids—our kids!

I started to feel lonely within our relationship. I tried to communicate more and tried to unsuccessfully get his attention about underlying problems that I felt were destroying our marriage. He failed to acknowledge this and instead suggested it was normal because we had been together for many years now. I was told I imagined things and invented scenarios in my head. Nothing changed. Maybe he was right--maybe I expected too much from a long-term marriage. Life went on, and we continued to go through the motions.

I became restless and started to dream of extra marital relationships, ones where I was loved and cherished. I would fantasize about past "mediocre" relationships which were not good, but not so bad compared to the present one. I even dreamt I divorced him! I was not proud of myself for this and even felt a little guilty. How could I think like that? He never abused or harmed me or the kids; he never cheated on me or done anything to deserve these negative thoughts! He loved his family as much as I did, and it was unthinkable that I could take this away from him and hurt him. I felt compelled to stay as we had a family together and lot of history too. To me, we were in this together until death do us part--divorce was not an option! The last thing on my list was to have a broken family. My family was my pride and joy, and I think like most women, I valued myself by it. It was a barometer of personal success.

Everyone was in awe of us, and we gathered compliments on our big family wherever we went. People would look upon us as a reference--look up to us and view us as such a beautiful romantic thing. A little voice inside was dying to say that it is not quite as beautiful as it appears from the outside because on the inside was a lonely non-supported woman who was dealing with multiple sources of pent-up frustration on many levels. Her partner was there physically, but he had detached himself emotionally from us all. He was living the life of a single guy in a family context.

The older kids started to notice the lack of love and caring, the emotional detachment, and the increased selfishness on his part. They would comment and complain. One of the children even stated she would never marry a man like this. His selfishness and egocentric traits were predominant, but he would glow in his narcissism at all the compliments he could recall about me and the kids. We became "trophies" to boost his huge ego. He became more and more controlling from family finances to what groceries I put into the shopping cart and even how I placed those groceries in that cart too!

Things became stifling. I asked for practical help, and he would evade to the yard work. He became hooked on the computer. The glass of wine became a bottle of wine, and he started to smoke.

When I fell pregnant with our seventh child in 2007, I thought this may be our last chance of togetherness. I hoped and prayed we could re-kindle the joy of adding a new recruit to our beloved family. We had always been closer than ever during my pregnancies, waiting for another miracle of life--another bundle of joy. However this pregnancy was void of all these things. I now realized what it was like to be a single pregnant mother. At a time in a woman's life where she needs her man more than ever, he was simply vacant. There was no emotional support or support of any kind--just me and my growing baby.

This pregnancy almost cost me my life. One morning half-way through my pregnancy, I awoke with stiffness and acute swelling of my leg, so I called myself an ambulance. I realized I had thrombophlebitis--a blood clot that travels with the blood-flow via a large vein, the kind that leads to the heart. I realized how fragile life was and how close I came to death. The rest of the pregnancy was spent injecting myself with blood thinners and having numerous tests. I could hardly walk in the earlier days, and I was profoundly disappointed that I was still not offered any help or support. At this point, it dawned on me that I could have died, and he did not care. I found myself crawling on all fours to do household chores, but still there was no compassion. "Was this supposed to be love?" I asked myself.

He would become short with me and even pick fights with no mercy. He would show no remorse at all. His answer to all now was, "We will stay together a few more years--then part." He meant if I wished, as I was the one visibly not happy. He stated that I was the one with the problem. He continued, "We will sell the house and go our own ways." There was no compromise or no efforts for reconciliation. Was this the ultimatum I was being given? Was this going to be a plotted cheap ticket "out" of our marriage for him?

I let it go, would cry myself to sleep, and still hang on to hope--hope for better days. I would tell myself no woman should be treated this way, least of all when she is emotionally fragile and pregnant and most in need of protection and support. The emotional distance between us grew larger and larger, and finally the gap became like a moat.

I could not help but think of all the wonderful men who were the husbands of the women who give birth at the birth center where I worked and had been working at for the past 10 years. How lucky they were. Why could I not have even a fraction of that love, care, and support? Was I not demanding enough?

Was it true? Like he had always said to me, I did not complain and whine enough.

He next decided he was going to make another career change in real estate. This took him away from the home in the evenings. Now, work by day and study in the evenings. The timing was bad, but who was I to complain? I had given up expecting anything by now. He even let me in on the possibility that he may not be there for the birth as he had exams scheduled around my due date.

I also discovered the painful experience of giving birth with a father who was emotionally absent. Fortunately I was numbed, so I did not have to feel the pain--physical or emotional. He was not there, and nor was I. Fairness in the unfairness--a far cry from my other natural and home birth experiences. He was almost "moved" and almost shed a tear when our baby emerged; however, he was much more "present" and emotional for the births of his other children.

Our youngest was shown very little affection. It would rip my heart out. She would cry, I was busy in the "house of no help," and he would ignore her. I promised her I would love twice as much as I could not feel that love from him to her. I was the over-compensating parent and he consequently drifted further and further into the background taking very little parental responsibility.

This child, our seventh, a 7th blessing named Eden, as in the Garden of Eden, became my little garden of joy, my sunshine throughout the storm--my saving grace. Things were adrift. I knew I was not imagining it now. I wanted to get to the bottom of the problem. It was there--I could feel and smell it. My intuition was sending me messages, and I needed to hear the truth. Things could not go on like this. I was shutting up and closing down to my detriment.

I probed and questioned. I could no longer live with this indifference. We were living like two empty shells--he still claimed everything was okay and that he was just a little stressed due to his new job. I did not buy this, and I could see a lot of pain in his eyes. I could read his unhappiness. He would get irritated at my questioning and close up like a limpet. I was not going to go there. I don't think he was willing to go "there" himself.

He was now avoiding me, secluding himself in other rooms. The more I tried to get close, the more he would use any tactic to slip away into his own little world, a world of superficial stimulation, numbed on alcohol and nicotine--a world I did not belong to. He would stay up late. It seemed as if he was having a full-time relationship with his lap top...he had his own account now too. We had always shared everything up until now. I would stay up late, too, in a bid to collect a few more crumbs of love. He would alternatively go to bed early, and I would do the same—anything including watching the same television shows that I didn't care for just to be with him. I wanted him back, the guy I had married--the nice guy I used to know. I wanted us back!

Intimacy became rationed also. I could not understand how he had gone from being a very considerate and attentive lover to a cold inert body next to mine. The humiliation of being pushed away once too many times made me start to feel that there was something wrong with me as a woman. My whole femininity was under attack--the whole essence of being a woman was rubbished. I had to keep reminding myself of the compliments others had made about how my body was still good and all the remarks of disbelief when I told people I had seven children. This was my only anchor to maintaining my self-esteem. Why were none of these compliments coming from him anymore? Gone were the days when he was erotically attracted to me.

Throughout the years I had grown to accept that his libido was less developed than mine, but I knew this was a fact amongst many couples, so I just focused on his good points and put up with the rest. To me, there was more to a relationship than just sexuality, so I accepted this point. However, I would challenge him on his lack of sexual desire, and he would fob me off with the fact that he may have flagging hormones due to age. We were in our early 40's! I even asked him once if he was gay not really thinking this was an option because hey, he was married to a woman--to me--and we had seven kids together... not to mention the derogatory terms he used when talking about homosexuals. He laughed off the prospect of my questioning his being gay with a, "Maybe I am," said in a sarcastic tone.

Things became unbearable on the home front. His lack of love and respect for me was over spilling onto the now-teen members of our clan. Teenagers are not known for their compassion and with the role model of a father they had...well, I found myself going against the tide of things, trying to make things work solo. I became the whining witch who ended up closing down and giving up on the outside and on the inside! I did not recognize myself like this. This was not me.

I was not part of anything anymore. I was not invited to wine when we had his family stay as guests. I was feeling lost and lonely, walking around like a leper. I was not part of anything now, not even family photos. I was pushing down frustration, and my life felt like it was being robbed little by little. I was only allowed to cook and care for each and every family member, but who was caring for me? Who was I anyway? Where did happy-go-lucky Elaine go to? Did she burn herself out, did she not shout loud enough to be heard....did she die? It certainly felt this way because I had died on the inside. All basic human needs were denied. Fortunately I had the love of my children and good friends to pull me through. My inner light and my determination gave me the strength to carry on.

Communication was nil. He was pulling away. He no longer wanted to maintain friendships with family friends. He was distant with my family when they visited. Conversation was very business-like. Togetherness was a thing of the past, and he started to say strange things such as he was more of a bachelor kind of a guy, not really suited to a large family. He even started to comment on how nice men's bodies were while watching commercials on television. He began to work out more at the gym and buy himself more clothes even when finances were low. His new career in real estate required him to do long hours, often in the evenings and weekends which meant even less time for me and the kids.

He also started to shave the hair off his body. I would innocently say I didn't mind if he was growing hairier with age....little did I know he was not doing this for me!

All the decisions most couples make together were now made solely by him. Even our bedroom make-over decor was chosen alone. It was now *his* bedroom. Even if my money helped pay for it, what was "mine was ours," and what was "his was his."

One day, the day before April Fool's Day in 2008, I had taken way more than I could and should have taken. I was at the end of my rope, and something had to give. I wanted out, but I had nowhere to go. I was leaving. I made supper and took my two youngest kids with me as I knew he was working the next day and the kids had school; therefore, our pre-schoolers would have nobody to care for them. As I left, Francois looked at me angrily and exclaimed, "You are ridiculous!" He added, "Maybe we could talk about it." *Hello*...I had tried over the course of several years now!

I left, regardless, and all the other kids burst into tears. I reassured them I was coming back and not to worry. My heart sank. What am I doing? What am I doing to them? I felt compelled to leave. My eldest gave me a hug and asked me why. I told her I was not happy. She said, "I know mom!"

I drove around in the dark, tears pouring down my face. I could hardly see where I was driving. I did not know where I was going, but I was going somewhere. The snow was falling, but at a slower rate than my tears.

We went for supper. I could not eat. "This is it," I was thinking, but it cannot really be, can it? The kids could feel my pain, and they were crying too. My body closed down; I was not able to breastfeed my youngest. My emotions had devoured me and my milk supply too. We paid and took off with everyone looking at us. I felt like the whole world knew I had walked out on my family. Was I being irrational, or was I going insane? I questioned.

We tried to sleep in the car, but it was too cold outside. Finally we spent the night in a motel. My five-year-old was confused as to why we were there. I was not sure how to explain. It was not long before they fell asleep, exhausted, huddled up to me in the same double bed. Their hearts beat to the rhythm of mine. My head throbbed with all the tears I had shed, and I finally fell asleep emotionally exhausted and drained.

The next day, we went home to an empty house. We tripped over the colossal mess. Nothing was cleaned from the night before, as I was not there. Even the pup had pooped around the house, and I was left to clear it.

I was so livid. I contacted my mother-in-law to fill her in on the fact things were not working out and that I had really had enough now. I didn't want to deal with her blame, so I felt I needed to justify myself. She was very understanding and said she would have a word with her son. I think because she is such an overbearing woman, and he was very careful not to disappoint her, she had more clout than me, so I felt it best left in her hands! I went upstairs and there I saw a letter on my bedside table. Oh, I thought--maybe he has come to his senses and wants to make amends.

I opened the letter, and as I read it, my whole body numbed over. I could not feel my limbs, I could not breathe...I felt as though I had been shot at point blank there in my bedroom. I could not think straight. Did I read it right? I read it over and over. I went into shock...my whole body went into shock. I was reading the words but could not make sense of it. It was like I was reading a foreign script. Was this some kind of joke--a sick one--on me?

I could not cry. I was numbed to the core. My feelings went into deep-freeze mode.

All day long I tried to make sense of it. I was so confused and kind of expecting Jeremy Beadle from the show "Game for a Laugh" to crawl out of the closet and say I was on camera!

My mother-in- law called back, giving me some advice. I told her of the letter. I told her that her son says he is gay. I felt sick to the gut. She cried and I cried. I could hardly speak. It felt so surreal.

Time stood still. I waited for him to come home. The wait was never–ending during which time I was dysfunctional. I could not eat, I could not do anything, and I was paralyzed with fear. I needed to hear the words because I could not digest them in written form.

My whole life flashed before me, and how could this be? Why me? What happened? Why did I fail to see this coming? What about all we had had together? Was this all in my imagination? What was real--what were lies...was my whole life a lie? Was I living someone else's lie?

I felt like I had not only been shot at point-blank but robbed also. Robbed of my identity. Robbed of the essence of my femininity, my dreams, and ideals. My life was like a carpet swiped from under my feet and at such speed that I did not see it coming. Had I fallen into the black hole of illusion?

Part of me was relieved. Finally we had a "diagnosis" to this long-term illness. It was him and not me! He finally came home, but the wait was excruciatingly long. I first asked what makes him think he is gay. He confessed to an encounter with a man he had met via the Internet a few weeks back. But he insisted it was just a *curiosity* thing and that he is not gay--he said it was not true--and I should destroy the letter! Now I was totally thrown because he was retracting from this huge blow. How could somebody write something so profound and compelling, then wish to retract and say it was not true? Something deep inside said to hang onto the letter for future reference. I did just that. The letter accompanied me for a whole year. I would gauge my hurt level every time I read it. It became my pain yardstick. Things became clearer and clearer the more times I read it. I knew its contents by heart. When it no longer hurt me, I put it away.

I had so many questions and so few answers. I wanted to piece together this broken puzzle piece by piece. I wanted to believe that he may at least be bisexual to preserve half of him. He shared his story regarding the guy that he had met. It was someone online, and he had used a work real estate appointment as an alibi. According to him, they had indulged in mutual pleasuring, but I was not to consider it serious as it was a "one-of thing." He also added it was purely physical and therefore "nothing in it," and it was with a guy, so therefore it was not cheating. He promised not to do it again and asked for my forgiveness.

Now I was left with feelings of distrust. Was this a "one-of" thing as he suggested or has this been an on-going thing that I have been oblivious to? He also mentioned there was no passion in our relationship anymore. Was I being blamed for his cheating now? He went on to say that I was a beautiful person inside and out, and any man would be happy to have me in his life. He went on to say he would never do this with another woman as no woman is better than me. This left a bitter-sweet taste in my mouth. How was I to take these back-handed compliments? What good were they to me now? In the latter years, I never really felt valued for my true worth. He seemed proud to have me in his life when others complimented me.

I suggested he was confused and we needed to work on our marriage. In hindsight, I was equally confused. He agreed, and we took an appointment with a couples' therapist. She said it was a serious matter and told him to tell the truth, the truth, and the whole truth.

He claimed he regretted what he had done and wanted to work things out in his marriage because he still loved me and wanted us to stay together. That sounded just what I wanted to hear, so I plunged into to denial right there and then. Like a skydiver from a plane, my parachute of hope re-opened and I was going to do all it would take to get us back on track.

However, deep down and buried, I was wondering how I could forgive the unforgiveable...forget the unforgettable.

We had a family trip planned to Florida that summer, so we tried to get things back on track. It was to be our first overseas holiday together as a family, and the added bonus was that my sister and her family who lived there were going to be with us as well as my mum and aunt who would fly in from the United Kingdom. It would be one huge family reunion. How great would that be!

Things between us were better than ever. We both worked on our relationship with guidelines from the therapist. Things felt so real and alive again. He was being everything he used to be, and everything I wanted him to be--loving, caring, and passionate. We kind of relived a sort of honeymoon phase, both of us basking in denial and hanging onto the last threads of hope.

Once home from holidays, routine and the old-grind set in. He was less and less willing to make those promised efforts to salvage our marriage. I was in denial, and although I had tried to forgive him, the vase was broken and I knew deep, deep down, deeper than my denial that it was over.

Later he confessed now that he had a taste of homosexuality, it was hard for him to refrain. He said he was not sure after all if he could abide by therapist's guidelines of getting our marriage back on track. He said he did not want to leave me as he loved me and the kids, but he needed a man to feel fulfilled. He said he would be okay if I allowed him to have relationships a few times a month with men. He assured me there would be nothing in it as it would be purely sexual. So adamant was I to keep my family intact, I almost gave this option consideration until I realized it was all so against my integrity. None of this was part of me or my wedding vows. Why was I even considering it? This was not my idea of a family. What message and values would we be transmitting to the kids? What was going to be in this for me? Had I really lost all sense of self to the point that I was going to sacrifice me for him? I found myself struggling as if I was on a tight-wire of hope, hanging on for dear life as I was thrashed by dashed hopes and dreams.

A few weeks later, after asking me to keep all this news to myself, (the burden was huge) I was now the one in the closet. Meanwhile he became more and more obsessed with the computer, and I suspected him of soliciting gay websites. Not long after this, he coldly announced he had met someone and was moving out. This other married gay man with a wife and two kids was now willing to move out also. He had promised his wife never to leave if she allowed him extra marital sex with men, but he changed his mind. My world fell apart.

When he finally came out to the kids, they all reacted in different ways according to their personalities and age. He announced it to some, going by age group, and he laughed as he came out to them. They came to me thinking it was a joke. My eldest knew before the others as she had been home at times when I would melt-down. I told the younger ones myself.

Some lost all faith in relationships; others were too ashamed to tell their friends, and if they did, they said their father had left for another woman. They were all confused by this almighty blow. Although the kids had been raised in an environment of compassion and understanding of anyone who was different-- we never hid our gay friends' sexuality--it was different now. We were talking about their father. They now had to consolidate a new reality with the one they thought they knew. Their father had become a stranger to them as much as he had become one to me.

My only son was gutted. He was the only male in the household now. His father and role model had disappeared overnight. Their family, the only family they knew, had folded up before their very eyes. No one is more vulnerable than the children innocently born to gay/straight parents. I felt a pang of guilt, that I had chosen him to be their father. They deserved better than this. I wanted to wrap them in a huge blanket and protect them from this pain--the pain, the shame, the stigma...none of which belonged to them. I did not want them exposed to his homosexual-lifestyle. They were not ready for this. I was over-protective towards them, and homosexuality wrecked my marriage. I did not want it to wreck my kids too. He expected that once he was out, we and the whole world would be okay with it. The fact it took him forty-odd years to be okay with it was irrelevant.

It would rip my heart out to see my little one, still in diapers, run to the door every time someone came home. She would call out "papa" in the hopes that she could see him. Her older sister of six years would console her with a hug saying, "Papa will never come home again."

He walked away from half of our lifetime together. He was choosing some stranger he had known for a couple of weeks over us...me and his kids. I could not wrap my head around this reality. Back into shock I went. My life was becoming like a soap opera. I did not know him anymore. I felt scared and intimidated having him around. I would wake in the night wondering who this guy next to me was. Was I worth anything anymore? I felt as though I had been discarded like a bag of garbage dumped on the curbside...used, abused, and violated. I begged him not to divorce me--what did I do wrong? Was I not worthy of keeping the marriage together? The stigma of it was huge for me. I asked myself over and over what I did wrong until one day it dawned upon me that his homosexuality had nothing to do with me.

He was always known as a decent, honest sort of guy. All I could see was deceit, double deceit...he became a traitor to me. In the meantime, he was skipping around like a love-struck teenager, showing me pictures of his new "love" talking about him openly around the dinner table in the presence of the kids. He would also sneak out to talk to him on his cell phone, go out for "boys' nights out," and leave me to care for the kids. He would come home and tell me every sordid detail about how good it was with a man. I had to pinch myself as I was numbed to the core. I felt nauseous. My life was a living nightmare. He would also add insult to injury by typing love letters to him on his lap-top as I sat beside him on the sofa.

He spent the next few weeks checking out and buying second-hand furniture via the computer. House hunting, he was ready to take off. We had not discussed a thing.....he was planning to walk out of the door and out of our lives for the life he felt he should be living. His new life began. My life ended.

He told me I was strong, and things were not so bad as our eldest were teenagers now. Therefore I only had the "younger ones to really care for." Anyone who has parented to her or his full capacity knows just how untrue this is.

He had always been the one to take care of bills, bank accounts, and most family finance matters. Now I had no choice but to handle them myself. I felt totally overwhelmed by this prospect. I barely knew what a mortgage was. This was an extra burden for me.

He tried to normalize things by telling me that lots of couples split and many kids have broken homes so, "Get over it."

I never once felt he could feel my pain. He did not want to know how I felt or how I was going to deal with it all. He even invited me to have supper with his new boyfriend, the boyfriend's wife, and their two young sons. I was emotionally crippled in his newfound happiness. He was oblivious to the pain he had caused. He angrily and sharply told me to keep my anger to myself when I declined the supper invitation. Did he really think I was going to make a tea party out of this whole sadistic affair? I was not even allowed to my own feelings now; he wanted to control and take possession of them too.

He would come home and announce he loved Claude, his boyfriend, and did not love me anymore. This was another shot to the heart. Other times he would say he could not make up his mind whether he wanted to stay with me and his kids or leave. I was walking around feeling sick to the gut. He was just walking away from it, leaving me the whole burden--the whole package deal.

I could not eat because my emotions were stuck in my throat. Nothing would go down. I lost 15 pounds overnight, and then he told me I was unattractively skinny and needed to put on some weight. I was unable to think straight. I started to suffer from anxiety attacks and just could not stop crying. Every time I was in a safe place to do so, he told me coldly and heartlessly to go see a doctor and be put on anti-depressants. I would often try to hold everything in, but then the dam would break. Tears would slide down my cheeks. I could not stop them. I cried like I had never cried before. These tears calmed my anxiety and my fears. Months and years of pent-up anger and frustration burst forth, and all the interior pain spewed out.

Who could I talk to about this? Whoever would understand? I had never, never felt so alone. I just wanted to cry in somebody's loving arms like a child who wanted its mother. I wanted to be in a safe place. I wanted to go back home. For the first time in a longtime, I wanted to go back to my hometown to be with my first family and to be with my mum.

It took me time to process and understand it all before I was willing to share fully with others. I found solace with people I did not know. I started to contact people on internet. That way I did not have to show emotions as I sat behind my computer screen. I even used this form of communication to go on coffee dates in a secret bid to see if I was worth anything anymore. Once my doubts were resolved, I ran away from the scary prospect of being intimate again. I decided I needed to heal alone for a while.

I started to volunteer in our local hospice. It kind of put my own life in perspective and enabled me to operate from the heart and forget my own blahs for the while I was there.

I sought out therapy. This helped me greatly to re-find a sense of myself and prepare for separation; however, it felt as though there was a huge part the therapist was unable to grasp. She just could not reach me. Due to no fault of her own, how was she expected to understand--it did not happen to her body! She had not been "there"--there was a huge void. I found an online group therapy. I felt for the first time that someone had come the closest to really understanding my pain.

Life continued. Francois would go to work as if nothing had happened and make excuses why I was not able to go to social functions with him. He never told anyone he had a new partner and he was leaving me. He even suggested his family in France did not need to know. I was sworn to silence.

I suggested he get therapy, but he said he didn't need it. He was "out" but still living a double life. I was left feeling battered and beaten beyond compare. How was I going to get my aching body through all this? Who would want me, a middle aged woman with seven kids? He had stolen my better years, and I was left for dead. All of this in the name of love. What was going to happen to me? I was overwhelmed with fear. I was in a cloud of gloom. I felt worthless, beaten down, and useless. I thought I was living one reality, but it was all an illusion. I felt like I had been cheated on for all of my married life. His hidden homosexuality was his "mistress" of many years.

I continued therapy, and the therapist made me aware of the obvious. She asked why he was still doing all this, putting me through so much emotional distress and still living at home. In my confusion and with my irreproachable fidelity, he said he has nowhere else to go. With this, she said he is thinking of himself only and he must go as soon as possible. She said I was internalizing too much stuff, and it was unhealthy for me. I went home, mentioned this, and he moved out the next day. He left, offended that I never gave him more time to find an apartment. He left true to himself, thinking of nobody but himself.

Some of my kids were upset as they thought I had kicked their poor father out. He somehow became the victim. I tried to explain things to them as best I could without making them feel they were in the middle of things. Those that were willing, I got into therapy in a bid to make things clearer for them to grasp. I could barely comprehend it, so I could just imagine their profound confusion.

He moved out and moved in with his new boyfriend. He walked out of the door, leaving a derelict home and derelict hearts behind him. He just closed the door on half a lifetime together. I was left to pick up the pieces. I was living my own personal tsunamis. I was dealing with my own pains and the fall-out from each and every one of the children—and it was huge. I just wanted to protect their little injured souls. In their confusion, some took their anger out on me. I was the last wounded soldier standing to bear the brunt--the strongest donkey on the trail that carried the heaviest load on its back!

My nights were disturbed like never before. I had become a total wreck. If only I could go to sleep and not wake up again. But I had to keep up a brave front for my kid's sake I had to hold down my jobs x 2 which ended up as x 3. As the financial burden also set in, I became the primary source of income too. The shame I felt--I wished I would not have to go through the added pain of feeling this shameful truth. It was a nightmare I could not wake up from.

I started to avoid calls from my friends and family and turning down invitations. I became a recluse. It was easier not to see anybody that to let them see me suffer. I was embarrassed to tell anyone too, especially those nearest and dearest to me. When I finally did tell people, some of their comments were very hurtful. Amongst them I was asked often if it was worse to be cheated on for a man or a woman. Pain is pain; infidelity is infidelity .their impact is the same. There is no difference. I was being bombarded with the very questions I was asking myself. Some assumptions on other's behalf were also very hurtful.

"Maybe you did not love him enough," was thrown my way and received like a slap in the face. Or there were accusing comments like, "How on earth did you not know?" I was stuck in a maze of confusion. My mind was in limbo. He was stepping off the sinking ship leaving me shipwrecked. I was resentful towards him. How dare he just walk away? Surely this was a crime.

After he moved out for the "love of his life," one whole month later he was back on my doorstep. They had parted. He came into the house and broke down on one occasion. I was touched to realize he did actually have feelings. I could only see him as a callous monster by now. He showed no remorse for his actions; it was all about him. I was still expecting an apology that just never came. I realized that I just needed not to expect anything from him anymore. If he could do all this to us, he could do anything. I was not expecting anything good from him now that he was out. His tears were of self-pity; however, he was crying as he thought his kids and family would be ashamed of him. It was still all about him. I would have liked him to ask how I was. He never did. He did not want to know.

Months passed. He clearly wanted to come back as he now realized he could not afford to be paying rent. His partner was no longer around to pay. He had lost it all now, and he was clearly lost.

As if going trough emotional turmoil was not difficult enough, I was also thrust into financial famine. I was now receiving threatening letters from hydro and electricity companies and court for numerous accumulating unpaid bills. Everywhere I went I was hounded for unpaid debts. I felt like an animal tracked down and hunted for kill. Sometimes I just felt like going to sleep and not waking up again. This was huge-- larger than life.

Every time I dared to ask for some financial support, I was told he didn't have any money. I was passive-aggressively hung up on over the phone, and doors closed in my face when I tried to ask him for child support. We had some emotional blackmail thrown in too; he was now threatening suicide. I was told to stop complaining and be content with what I have got as if he takes his life, I (we) will really know what hardship is all about. None of the practical help he had offered when he left materialized, and he would hardly see the kids.

Unfinished do-it-yourself jobs around the house were left unfinished and were possible danger/health hazards to the kids.

He went on to borrow and pilfer money from the kids. My debit card disappeared during my absence (trip back to England). Just to add insult to injury, he spent my money at a gay bar after paying off all his debts with it.

Later that year he had a drunk-driving ticket and huge fine, and so not only was he unable to support us financially, he was now exempt from any parental responsibility.

From the day he left in 2008 to this day, after relentless efforts and visits with a mediator, I am still not receiving a cent from him. I have two jobs and have had to work lots of overtime—sometimes—60-hour weeks to just survive. The mortgage is left unpaid, and we have the further stress of possibly losing the roof over our heads. From time to time he appears with various forms of emotional black mail, asking for money from me and the kids claiming that poverty is affecting his health. What about mine? What about me? What about us? The walking wounded left behind. I have not had one word of thanks or recognition for everything I have done and paid for. I am holding down the fort alone.

I did not seek out a lawyer as I needed every penny I earned. He walked out and did not have the decency to allow me to have closure. Mediation proved a challenge as he was clearly not willing to co-operate. He wanted to still be the one calling the shots. Play it by his own rules--the only rules he knew.

I am still not divorced. It is hard not to be angry. I am a woman of compassion, so I will admit I do still have compassion for him. But I have to learn to have compassion for myself also...I am working on that!

The kids get upset because while he was out and living his life. He was getting lifts from them even to gay bars. (He lost his car due to a drunk-driving fine that caused him to lose his license and pay a huge fine) They never heard from him unless he needed them. They were hurt beyond words. I tried to explain to him that the fact he was gay is not a choice but being a responsible father is. He never allowed them to slowly accept this new reality that he was gay. Instead he thrust his gay lifestyle on them. My eldest daughter had the shame of a gay client recognizing her father on business cards at her workplace stating he saw "that guy" on a gay website. Others were exposed to indecencies either live or on the computer. There was a general lack of privacy with his private life.

I was on the emotional roller-coaster and went through each stage of bereavement bit by bit...dealing with each emotion as it hit me in the face. The only way out of this dark tunnel was to go through it. I went step by step, taking my inner-light with me to guide me through. My inner strength and outside support helped to get me through this. I was not going to give up or give in; I was going to get "me" back. I promised me all the love and caring I had given to others and not to myself. All the love and respect I did not get from others, I was going to give to me first. I was going to get better--not bitter. I was going to be a winner-- not a loser.

Regardless of the huge pain, there was, however, an element of joy and relief. Finally, we had some kind of prognosis to this long terminal illness of a marriage. It was him, not me. I no longer had to ask what my part was in all this.

I found myself going into mental trances remembering each detail of my marriage and relationship to this man that I did not know anymore. He had become a total stranger in his new life now--a life I was no longer part of. How was I ever to trust or love again? Whose shoulder was I going to cry on? The very person I would turn to in times of disaster and personal crisis, my number one resource person on this continent—him--had now turned into the cause of my pain.

Twenty years of marriage was to be dissolved; half of my lifetime frittered away. The future that is left is so full of scars now. Deep wounds, wounds of confusion and pain. I am now bereft of the mate I thought I had for a lifetime.

He asked to be my friend. My friends do not treat me this way. I did not want a friend—I wanted a husband and a father to my kids. I now had not only to contend with the news that my husband is gay but also now being left as a single parent with broken dreams and a broken marriage. He was the closest person to me and has become little more than a stranger to me. I thought he was my friend; I never thought for one minute he would be capable of treating me so poorly. I wanted to be cared for, for the rest of my life.

I innocently entered a damaging situation which has created profound trauma on many levels. Trust has become a big issue for me now--not only the trust of others, but trusting my own judgments too. How could I have made such a big mistake? I realize that you can never really truly know someone. He has no clue as to the damage he has caused his family. To think he promised to love, cherish, and respect.

Update on me now!

I am in a better and safer place in my life now. We have no control of our past, but we have control of our future happiness. Life is full of good and bad experiences, and we learn and grow from them. I have become whom I was supposed to be also. He chose himself and I choose me now. I have learned to take full control of me and my life now. I will no longer wrap myself around anyone else. I re-build my life for me, the way I want it! I have learned to let go and to believe in myself and trust myself. I have a stronger sense of "I." It was important for me to open up the pressure cooker of emotions and deal with each and every one at my pace until they perished and I let them go.

Anger finally left my body and was replaced by acceptance. Then slowly but surely the negative emotions were replaced by the positive ones--those of joy and happiness. My experience has changed many things about how I see myself and how I look at life. I decided I needed to take time for me and be in a relationship with myself, regain trust and confidence, rediscover the *lost* me, be as kind to myself as I am with others, and not give anything to others that I do not first give to myself in terms of love and respect. I realized how much I had self-sacrificed to keep my marriage intact. Nobody should self-sacrifice for others in this world. We should all be masters of our own lives, our destiny, and make ourselves the most important person in our lives. We need to be our own best friend.

It has been a long process to get where I am now in my life. I am at peace with my past. I am happy now. I have finally escaped the prison of shackled emotions. I am no longer hanging onto false hope. I can have real hope now. I knew I had to let go. I had to allow the sincere tears of an adult to fall on the cheeks of a woman who was not allowed to be. These tears calmed my anxiety and fears. We have to go beyond our deepest fears to find true happiness. We need to hold onto faith.

I have learned to love myself; I do not wish to depend on others to love me in a way that can be disappointing and defeating because ultimately I love myself. Some things happen to us from which we never really fully recover. But we must accept and welcome the 'new normal' life which will never be the same, but the sooner we accept the way things are the sooner we can live in peace with the new normalcy!

I believe things happen for a reason even if we are not always clear as to what that reason is at the time. There are messages we must pick up on. A few months back I went to change my vehicle number plates, and the lady handed me a number plate with number "1" on it. I was taken aback! "Can I keep this plate forever?" I asked her nervously. Now I drive around with that plate with great pride and joy! I couldn't have picked a better one if I had tried. So now I make that my mantra--that plate is for me! The message is, "I am Number 1 in my life now!"

I remain positive and try to see an advantage to every situation. I now see there was no happiness to be had for either of us. There were no winners. And if finally you are happier out of a relationship than within, then answer is evident as to where we should be! I look at all I do have in my life and not at what I do not have. I am truly blessed to have good health and a family: seven wonderful kids, good friends, and jobs of compassion that represent me.

I allowed myself to be emotionally abused. I take my responsibility of my part of the broken marriage. I do not take what does not belong to me. However I keep my heart free from hate. I continue to spread sunshine to others. I am now taking my own life back and have even found strength and a new level of confidence.

Part of my reason for sharing my story is to liberate myself. Going over my experience has not been easy, but paradoxically "therapeutic." The turning of the pages one by one, chapter by chapter has helped to give me closure. Hopefully my message will offer peace and words of comfort and reassurance and be powerful encouragement to others. I sincerely hope that my story helps other women who are lost in the darkness as I once was.

Bon voyage!

Love and hugs,
Elaine xox

Erin's Story

I'm a smart, successful, sassy, attractive woman and mother. I have to repeat this statement to myself multiple times a day to remind myself of these facts because I still CANNOT believe how I--OF ANYONE--could have been DUPED. My healing process has been a bumpy road of self-assessment and discovery. The pain fades, the beauty remains! I repeated this sentence while in labor with my first daughter. It was my manta allowing me to focus on the future beauty I was to behold and not of the pain I was experiencing. I have a picture of me smiling while holding back labor pains. I look at the picture and see a woman filled with so many emotions – fear, joy, pain…

I've looked in the mirror many times over the last few years and have seen the same woman looking back at me. I'm repeating the same manta today. But today the pain is emotional and not physical. I've spent time in a fog trying to determine why it happened to me. Why did I stay so long? What did I do to deserve this? And why, oh why, does it haunt me? Why did I cry for a love I never received? Why do I allow myself to be affected by it today? My moment of truth took a very long time to discover. Sometimes the truth is just too painful.

We met in college in 1990. We were paired together to work on joint projects for marketing classes. I was not immediately attracted to him, but as we spent time together, I began to see him in a different way. I was dating and living with a boyfriend who kept me more than sexually satisfied. The problem was the boyfriend didn't have any goals for a future. I found out Jeff was dating his high-school sweetheart. They had been dating for 5 years. Jeff and I continued to spend more and more time together. Our marketing group finished a big project and we all went out to celebrate. After a number of cocktails our feelings for each other came out. We talked about having – Sex – No Strings Attached. We made plans to meet, BUT when we met, neither of us could do it. We liked each other. We each ended our current relationships and began dating each other during March Madness 1991.

I had no idea my future husband was gay, although looking back, there were definitely some red flags. I never noticed any stereotypical gay tendencies. We actually argued about having gay friends. I was raised by a very liberal single mother. Our family had many gay friends and couples. I was extremely gay friendly. Jeff on the other hand was very homophobic (red flag). I remember one fight we had while dating about a "what-if" question. I asked him what he would do if he found out his best friend was gay. He said he would no longer be friends with him because he would fear the friend would hit on him. It started a nasty argument which ended with me throwing a glass of water in his face in disgust.

I remember him telling me about his sexual relationship with his girlfriend. He said he turned her down for sex a lot (red flag). When they did have sex it was mainly anal sex (red flag). He said he was uninterested in having sex with her. It made me feel like a better woman because I thought he desired me. He bought me flowers and was a perfect gentleman. He didn't pressure me for sex at all. We both wanted to get to know each other better.

I remember the first time we made love. We planned it – he was living with his parents – so we planned an afternoon when they were away at work. We went to his room and he bent down to pull flowers out of his closet for me. I leaned against him and stroked his hair he pulled away upset I had messed up his hair. I thought it was odd but brushed it off. Brushing off questioning gestures, comments and looks would become more a part of my life than I realized at that moment. I moved my hands away from his hair and started kissing him. I started to remove my clothes and let them drop to the floor. Jeff removed his clothes but folded them neatly and placed them on chair next to his dresser. Again I thought it was odd he would take the time to fold his clothes but I continued to look past the little signs. We proceeded to the bed and tried to make love. He was having problems keeping an erection. He went to the fridge to get some beer for us to calm our "first time" nerves. We were finally able to finish but he needed to do it from behind to perform. Looking back today, I should have noticed the RED FLAGS.

Our sex life got better but it was never great or anything to brag about. It lacked passion and intimacy. I remember getting Jeff a card about "How Good It Was!" I thought it would help him think he was and become a better lover. But he had so many other wonderful qualities I wanted in a partner. He had goals – he was smart, attractive, and easy to talk to. I liked his Dad and Step-Mom and they really liked me. I could see a future with him. Was sex really that important? He started a new job and we moved in together within six months.

Our nothing-to-brag-about sex life took a turn for the worse. Jeff had lots of excuses. I didn't do a good enough job of cleaning. "I'm not tired now but I will be tired in the morning." He always came home for lunch and made a sandwich. I would sit naked on the counter and ask him to have me for lunch. He would decline! This was our sexual relationship – I would ask and ask and beg and beg for sex and he would say NO. We would argue about it. I quit asking for it. I could only stand so much rejection. We would have sex maybe once each month. I needed and wanted to be desired. But he was more to me than just the sex. He asked me to marry him, and I said YES. I didn't realize at the time how much the lack of sex and intimacy would change my life – my self-esteem and sexual self-esteem.

I was 26 and he was 24 when we married at the Anchorage Museum in May 1993. It was a big beautiful wedding. The wedding night was another thing. I had to talk him into having sex on our wedding night. In looking back, this was another RED FLAG, but I had never heard of a gay man marrying a woman. Jeff had no gay tendencies I had ever heard about. My husband was a very neat and orderly person. He cooked, cleaned, did the laundry. He was very particular about his clothes and he ironed them every night before work. Not a hair out of place or a wrinkle in sight. He was Mr. Perfect. All my girlfriends teased me about what a great wife I had.

I now understand the tendency to be very orderly and clean had a lot to do with his internal struggle with his sexuality. If he could compartmentalize every aspect of his outer world, just maybe he could control his inner desires. I do believe he was born gay. If he could flip a switch and change his sexuality he would have done it years ago. I know he loved me very much but not in the way a straight woman needs to be loved.

Our main marital issues were sex and chores. He didn't give me enough sex or intimacy, and I didn't do enough chores. About three years into our marriage, I almost gave up and moved to Seattle with girlfriends. I actually would have, but I found out I was pregnant on my birthday Oct 31, 1996. I kept it from him, but I told all my girlfriends. I considered having an abortion.

Jeff and I started counseling. I decided to keep the baby and told him in the lobby of our counselor's office. It brought us together. He was so happy, and I became happy. We surprised our parents and grandparents for Christmas with the news we were expecting. It would be the first grandbaby for both his and my parents.

Mia was born June 17th. She was 5 pounds and 9 ounces. Perfect. Jeff was such a proud and good dad. I remember he had told me he didn't want a boy. I look back now and wonder if he was concerned he would pass his homosexuality to his son.

It was the summer of 2001--over 10 years into our relationship. I've always said if you don't know the answer to a question, "Just GOOGLE it." Little did I know GOOGLE would provide a clue to why my marriage lacked passion and intimacy.   Sitting at the computer that summer day I pulled up the internet and starting typing – www.g and the internet history pulled up.   Staring at me in the face was www.gay.com. WHAT – WHAT – WTF??? Jeff and I were the only ones in our home who used the computer. Our three year old daughter knew three letter words – CAT, MOM, DAD but not GAY.

I can still feel my heart sink and mind race as it did that afternoon. Today 10 years later it's filled with anger, pain and disappointment.

That summer in 2001 it was filled with confusion and bewilderment. If www.g pulled up gay.com what would www.a (adult friend finder), www.b, www.c.... I can't remember every website I found that afternoon. But I do remember confronting Jeff about the www.gay.com and the other websites that evening.

His explanation was he wanted the two of us to experiment with an open "lifestyle" and this was his way of doing research. And the CRAZY part is I believed him. Don't get me wrong--I questioned and questioned him. I told him if he was it was okay. I just needed to hear the truth. I wasn't going to judge him. Maybe trusting him was a protection mechanism. What woman would ever want to believe she had married a gay man? And anyone that has every read the newsletters from Bonnie Kaye would be able to tell you what happened next. Ah YES--the honeymoon phase. Jeff gave it his all that summer. It was the best and most frequent sex of our entire ten year courtship and marriage. It was a great summer. Jeff got a promotion. We bought a beautiful new home and found out we were expecting a new addition to our family.

It should have been a magical Christmas. But the shoe dropped one December evening out with friends. Chris, a man Jeff had introduced to me as a friend from work that summer, finally told me the truth. Chris explained he had grown to love me as a friend that summer, and I needed to know the truth. Looking back, I believe he was in love with Jeff and wanted me to go away. He told me he had met Jeff in January 1999 in an X-rated video store. They had exchanged glances while in the store and proceeded to exchange pleasantries though a hole in the wall (glory hole) in the back viewing area. The reason Jeff had introduced me to Chris in the summer of 2001 was so they could spend more time together while we were all out.

I sat there listening to Chris and looking at Jeff from across the room. Jeff could see the pain and horror in my expression and I could see the panic on his face. We left immediately and I screamed and yelled and hit and demanded he TELL ME. I was so ANGRY at him – I told him he could be honest with me. He told me about the others – the Pepsi truck driver, meeting strangers at Barnes and Noble but he never told me details. I cried myself to sleep and met Chris again for breakfast the next day. I needed to know more.

Chris explained Jeff was gay. He told me Jeff had cried on his shoulder many times about not being able to come out about who he really was. He was scared he would lose his job and his parents respect and his family. I was so confused. Jeff – GAY?? No Way–Bi–maybe, but he couldn't be gay. We were married, we had a daughter, and I was 36 years old and 4 months pregnant with our second child.

I'm not sure when my husband started sleeping with other men. Jeff never admitted what he did with the other men. He admitted he might be bisexual when I pressed him. He would tell me it was normal behavior and I would be surprised how many men were just like him. I asked if all men were just like him then how come it wasn't common knowledge. My husband would not come out or say the words, "I'm GAY," but I knew he was deep in denial and living in the closet. I stayed in the marriage for our children. It became a marriage of convenience.

We quit having sex, and he became much more careful about his transgressions. I was miserable in our marriage. I had repeated affairs to fill my desires to be wanted by a man, to be touched and cared for by someone. It was a "Don't Ask, Don't Tell" marriage. He let me do whatever I wanted and didn't ask or care. I poured myself into my work, kids, and friends. We just got back on the same emotionless, passionless, roller coaster ride of a marriage. I pushed him farther and farther out of my life. I went out without him, won exotic trips from work and took girlfriends instead of him. He said I hurt him, and we went to counseling to try and repair our marriage. But the "Elephant in the Closet" did not come out in counseling.

I wonder to this day why I continued to let him hide his homosexuality. We would only focus on the lack of passion and how I did not do a good enough job cleaning. I turned 40, quit having affairs, and woke up to the fact I needed and wanted more. It took me another year, but I finally said I cannot do this anymore in November 2007. I wanted to separate for 6 months and he agreed.

It didn't take him long to find another cover. He met and began dating another woman immediately. We were still living in the same home. They had a date the day I moved out of the house – January 6, 2008. He told me he was sorry to disappoint me by dating a woman and not a man. I was crushed! Was it really me he didn't want? Was he really a changed man? Was I not attractive, smart, and successful enough for him?

He introduced her to the kids within three weeks of us separating. I guess I should not have expected anything less from him. He actually told me three months after we separated that now that he was dating a younger, prettier, more successful woman who liked his politics and music and that he no longer desired to do the things he did when he was married to me. I laughed at him and said if it was that easy to turn off his attraction to men he would have long ago. Less than three months later while making a complete copy of the computers in our home, I found what I needed to prove to myself that I didn't turn my husband gay. And the new girlfriend was no better after 6 months of keeping him from doing the things he did when he was with me. There were all the downloaded gay porn pictures – time stamped and dated past and present.

If Jeff had been open about his homosexuality, I really do believe we could have been friends. But he is in such denial about his true sexual identity. Searching and searching for the right woman to keep him from wanting to act on his homosexual desires.   I truly believe in the beginning of these new relationships he actually thinks he has found the perfect woman and is cured.   But entering relationships with women without informing them of his past, his present, and their future is wrong.

Jeff is getting ready to marry a 26-year-old woman he has known for less than one year, and his future with her will be more of the same as I experienced with him. It's not a matter of "IF" she finds out--it is a matter of "WHEN."

What he did to me and is still doing to others is unconscionable and without excuse. But the same goes for me. I have no right to allow myself to be emotionally and financially abused, to make excuses for my ex and to continue to forfeit my self-respect. The pain fades and the beauty remains, and it's no longer my secret to keep anymore.

Gracie's Story

This is my story and how I perceive the things that have happened to me in the last 38 years of marriage and finding out I had married a man who turned out to be gay. August 1971 was what I thought was the greatest day of my life. I married a fellow teacher whom I loved so much. I grew up in the western part of the state and moved to the eastern part because of a teaching job offer. I met him on my first day of teaching as one of my non-teaching duties was to collect lunch money in the cafeteria. He was good looking and seemed quite nice.

Our first date was that December for the teachers' Christmas party. We enjoyed being together and started dating exclusively. By February we were engaged, and the following August we were married. Married life seemed fine. He was very busy with teaching and activities that he had as a high school band director. He was a church organist and choir director. Civic organizations were also part of his busy life. Looking back, we didn't spend a great amount of time together because of all of his activities. In the summers for 3 years we would go our separate ways as we were both pursuing Masters degrees at different universities which happened to be at opposite ends of the state. We had agreed no children until after we had both earned our master degrees. By the end of the summer of 1994, we had achieved that goal. We bought our first house in November 1975 and our first child, a daughter was born in January of 1976. Our second child, a son, was born in 1981, so we moved to a large house.

Things seemed great. We had two children, a big house, and both worked full time at jobs we loved being teachers. As the children got older, I became very involved in their activities such as scouts and band. My husband was involved with his activities, so he spent very little time with the kids and theirs.

Behind closed doors, our marriage was dysfunctional at least in my eyes. I was a virgin when we married .He told me he was also. The sexual filament definitely wasn't there. Being inexperienced in sex, I had nothing to compare it to. I came to realize over a period of time that our sexual intimacy was simply a physical motion that we went through so he could get some pleasure. Orgasm, what is that? Once he was satisfied, he rolled over and went to sleep. I truly felt like a sperm receptacle. I didn't enjoy having sex with him. It was just a marital obligation. Therefore, I never complained about the infrequency of having sex. I had low self esteem so I figured this was good as it got.

In March 2008, my life changed forever when I found evidence of his other life. I knew then that our relationship would never be the same. The house had a large room which had been a small family run store. We always referred to it as the "store room." The store room was his. He gave music lessons there and had all of his stuff in that room. His man cave so to speak. He was somewhat of a hoarder and had piles of paper, magazines, books, and music everywhere. When I walked into the store that day, I was wishing he would clean it up. I was so embarrassed when parents would come and sit in the store while he was giving their child a music lesson. His mess, I felt, was a reflection on me even though the stuff in the room wasn't mine. He had numerous filing cabinets in the store room, and I wondered if they were all filled and why he couldn't put some of his stuff in them. So I decided to look to see what was in them.

I was totally shocked as to what I found. The first drawer I opened had all kinds of books about gays. Titles included "The Life and Legacy of Al Parker Gay Superstar," "My First Time-Gay Men Describe Their First Same-Sex Experience," and "My First Time Volume 5" as well as many more books. I opened another drawer and there were VHS tapes and DVD's all dealing with dealing with gays. There was even a drawer with the gay centerfolds that he had taken out of gay magazines that he read. Further searching lead me to a small notebooks with 18 pages of gay web sites and passwords.

I was overwhelmed beyond words. How could I have lived with this person for 38 years and had no clue? I couldn't confront him as I had no idea how to handle the situation or what to say. I decided it would be best to say nothing for the time being as our daughter was finally pregnant after numerous tries and I didn't want to upset her and I knew she would be devastated too. So began the heaviest burden in my life to carry. I was aware that he spent a lot of time on his computer and sometimes would quickly click out of the web site that he was on if I came into the room, but I had no clue as to what he was doing or watching.

From that time on, I became very much aware of what was going on around me. I became aware of how much porn mail and advertisements were coming to our home and the hours and late hours that he was spending on the computer. I decided to check credit card statements, and this was another shock. He was spending about $375 a month on porn materials and visiting pay-for-view web sites. After spending time going through credit card statements from 2002 to 2008, I found he had spent over $29,000 on his porn addiction. Still I said nothing. I decided to wait to confront him until after our son graduated from graduate school in May 2009. I didn't feel he needed to know this until after he graduated. So for the sake of my adult children, I decided to say nothing. The burden became heavier.

In July 2009, I found a paper with a dialogue between him and a person who turned out to be a gay man he had met on the internet. He typed to the young man "We'll most likely remain together officially if for no other reason than the pending debut of a grandchild (courtesy of daughter and husband) in January." I wondered why someone would print out an internet dialogue. Was I meant to find it? I found out that the young man was about 23 years old. He was 62. He traveled across the state to meet this person. He told me he was going to a music meeting and put it on the calendar as such. I had always trusted him including doing our banking. If the bank statements came in the mail, I just put them on his pile of mail unopened. Even when banking became available on line, I didn't check the status of our accounts. Well that was before I found the discovery in the "store room."

I checked our home equity our account and found we owed more than $13,000 on it. For what? I had no clue as we hadn't done any home improvements nor had we bought any big item purchases. I told him that I would help him pay it off over the next year and then he could pay me back. He agreed. Once the amount was very small we went to the bank to close the account. He was surprised when I told the bank we wanted to close the account. He thought we were just going to pay it off and leave it open. A true piggy bank for him was taken from him.

Finally in July 2009, after waiting from March of 2008 when I discovered his secret, I decided to confront him. Before I did, I had leased an apartment near my daughter who lives about 100 miles away. I had discreetly begun to go through my things and started packing for the move. I told him we needed to talk and asked him to take a seat at the kitchen table where I sat across from him. Here is the letter I handed him to read. I said nothing more till he finished reading the letter. It said:

The day I married you was one of the happiest days of my life. I was so much in love you and looked forward to spending our lives together forever. I thought we shared the same dreams and ideals of marriage. However over time, our ideals of marriage seem to have become very different. I feel marriage is about commitment, fidelity and trust. I have seen things change in our relationship and the love I thought we shared. I feel that I have been fulfilling your needs as a caregiver and social partner. I have contributed a second income and created a comfortable home for you. I feel that our relationship is one of content for you. Your basic needs are taken care of- meal preparation, laundry and cleaning. We have come to a point where we barely communicate as we have very little in common to share. This has lead to feelings of loneliness for me. We don't share or enjoy activities together and I've become unhappy with this situation. I feel you have become emotionally disconnected from me. Your emotions have turned elsewhere, your heart and mind are not focused on our relationship. We all make choices in life and are held accountable for those choices. As I see it, you have made on-line and off-line choices based on your sexual orientation, thus excluding me from your life. It is an insult to me each time I see you viewing your homosexual porn on your computer or climbing the stairs late at night after one of your viewing sessions. Your porn addiction consumes a great deal of your time and money. As a result of all of this, you are being disloyal to me and our marriage. Your life style and actions have eroded our relationship beyond repair. What you have done and continue to do have affected our lives and our love for each other. Our marriage is no longer a marriage simply by definition. We are just clinging on to what we wished we had. Things have changed and it's time to go our own ways before the good times and memories we shared get buried under any more resentment and hurt. Therefore I cannot remain in such an unloving environment. It's time I think of myself and my need for happiness. I am in the downhill of my life and I've worked hard and deserve better that what I have now. I've always put family first and now it's time to put me first for the years I have left on earth. I too have made a choice after much thought and consideration. I need to separate from you as I will not accept the closet as my home. We both need to be happy in our own lives and now is the time for us to change our lives and find happiness. Perhaps we can be better friends than spouses.

I observed him reading it, and he showed no expression or emotion. When he finished he said that I had it wrong, but when given a chance to explain he said nothing other than perhaps he might be bisexual. I told him I was moving out at the end of the month to be near our daughter and family. He said nothing. I said I wanted a divorce, and he said we could just tell people that we decided to go our own ways.

Within a few days of the confrontation, I shared my plan with my son about the moving and divorce .I asked him if he knew about his father's activities and he said he had been aware of the gay porn on the internet for a while. He didn't tell me as he thought I knew. I told my daughter and son in law. They were aware that things were not good between us, but had no idea about his secret life and gay porn addiction.

The effects of his secret gay life and addiction have been devastating to me. I was shocked to find the items in the drawer in the store as well as all the money he was spending on the internet and then the going off and meeting gays under false pretence. I felt so deceived by someone I had loved and had given the best 38 years of my life to. Until I opened the drawer in the store, I never had a clue. Yes, it is possible to live with a gay person and not know it.

I rented a small two bedroom apartment not far from where my daughter lived which was in a suburb of Philadelphia. I thought I would get support from her, and I wanted to be near my small grandson. I left a small town where I had lived for 28 years and the friends that lived in that town. I came to realize that moving wasn't the greatest idea. I didn't get the support I thought I would from my daughter, and the living was so much more expensive there, not to mention the large population of the area. I basically knew no one. I had no clue how to get to places. Thank heavens for a GPS. I was so stressed out. I had moved from a familiar surroundings and friends; I was in the process of getting a divorce and I had no one to turn to for support or help. I wished I was dead.   It was the most terrible time of my life. I truly didn't want to live. I was very lonely as I had never lived on my own. I also became depressed about my whole situation. I would have never considered suicide as I feel that would have meant he won. I decided I had to make the best of my situation remembering it's not what happens to you, it's how you react to it that matters.

I decided that in October I would return to my small town once my lease ran out on the apartment at the end of July 2010. I would go back to familiar surroundings and friends but until then I would become involved in my surroundings. I decided to volunteer at a large local hospital. I worked in the nutrition department office and loved it. The staff was great to work for and appreciative of the work I did for them. It helped make me feel that I was needed and valued. I also volunteered at a nearby theater as a daytime usher. I enjoyed that job too. I turned to God and found friendship in a local church. I joined two of their groups.

While living away, I did make a few visits back to my former home. I was permitted to stay there by him. We were separated then but not divorced. On one of my return visits I encountered a young man in the living room of our home. I'm not sure who was surprised more. He said he was there because his aunt had died and he needed comforting. He was about 23 years old. I asked his name and he told me. It turned out he was watching a very large flat screen television which I found out later that my husband had bought at a cost of over $1200 along with a 360 X-Box.

Over time, the young man has received designer clothes, a dog, plane ticket to Europe, monthly rent being paid for an apartment' and a BMW that was purchased in the ex's name to be driven by the boy toy. Wow I had never gotten anything like those gifts. Shall we say Sugar Daddy! It's too bad that so much money is being spent on this young guy. It's money the ex really doesn't have to spend. I don't think he has a clue to the cost of keeping this young guy, maybe someday he will. However, it's none of my business. Sex comes with a hefty price tag for some.

Our divorce was final in January of 2010. We each kept our own retirement funds and other financial assets. The only thing we had in both names was the house. It was appraised, and I was given half the value by him. It was very cut and dry.

In the summer of 2010, I returned to the small town I had once called home and purchased a small house, nothing like the large house I had lived in for 28 years. The important thing is that it was mine. The mortgage that came with it was also mine. Never in my wildest dreams would I have thought that at age 61, I would be taking out a mortgage to buy a house and start my life all over. I have put a lot of love and time along with some money to make my new (new to me) house into a home where I can find comfort, and my children can come and feel at home as well. Home is where your mother is.

As far as activities for me, I have become a member of the senior citizens with a group of retired former teachers. The bus trips are great. I also helped form a church group similar to one of the ones I belonged to in the Philly area. I have been a part of a group that has started a town museum. I have spent many hours working on displays for the grand opening this coming Labor Day weekend. My new life is under way.

As for my ex's and my current relationship, we talk when necessary. We recently were involved in our son's wedding so that did require some major communicating. He is in the process of selling "our house" and buying a smaller house in another part of town. Just last week I was helping our son remove his things from the house and the mood was very civil. The talking I wish he would do is to apologize for what has happened to us and our children. I realize being gay is not his fault as I feel a person is wired that way. It's not something they would choose. However, I still feel he owes me a big apology for deceiving me for all those years, hiding behind me to keep his secret and the demise of our family. He has never shown any regret. I feel he is still in denial.

I wish for other women who find themselves in a similar situation to be able to find resources and the support they need. I didn't have the necessary resources or the support I needed when I went through the year of hell. Only recently have I found a support group where I can go and share my feelings with other in similar situations. The first book I found was "My Husband is Gay" by Carol Grever. It made me aware that there were others out there in my same situation. I have found the books of Bonnie Kaye also very helpful especially the one titled Bonnie Kaye's Straight Talk and Straight Wives: Shattered Lives. I learned I wasn't the only one who had a gay husband who tore my life apart.

As for now, unfortunately I am still in the closet as is the ex. In a small town I don't feel comfortable sharing my situation with others. I know the ex hasn't told anyone, not even his only brother who is the only family he has. By not being able to tell others, I know I haven't received the support I should have gotten. I can only hope someday I will be able to get out of the closet but for now I just have to deal with it the best I can. I feel I did nothing wrong except marry a man I was very much in love with who had a dark secret and who happened to be gay.

Lily's Story

To the Reader: I am hoping that as I tell my story you, sweet reader, will be encouraged on your path to wholeness.

I am 57 years old as I sit to write this. Most people think I am much younger. I am small, in good shape, dynamic, and love God with all my heart. I am the Children's Ministry Director at my church; however, for 30 years I was a pastor's wife.

My story begins with one of my earliest memories – mother washing me in the bathtub and me jumping up and down screaming. I didn't realize until much later in life that what she did was a form of sexual abuse. I remember thinking to myself when I my daughter was born, "I would never do that to her!" When I later asked my two sisters if our mother had washed them like that they said, "No"; however, my older sister remembers me screaming.

Mother repeated to me all the time while I was growing up how I was unplanned, a mistake, and how she would fall down the stairs and jump up and down on purpose to try to miscarry me. "But you stuck" she would say in an ugly sarcastic voice. I grew up feeling like I didn't belong in my family and that I shouldn't even exist. I felt that she hated and resented me.

By the time I was four years old I laid outside in the grass and told God I didn't need my mother, I just needed my Dad. I vowed that when I grew up all my children would know they were wanted and loved no matter if they were planned or not and that they were here for a purpose.

So I started life with a deep gaping wound I knew nothing about. I just felt less than--always keeping a together appearance but underneath I was insecure, fearful, ashamed, empty, constantly fighting off the deep, egregious messages of the mother, not ever letting her know how she was hurting me. It wasn't safe. And even though I knew my father loved me, he was a deeply angry man who drank a lot, beat us a lot, and yelled at us a lot.

I was in survival mode all growing up. So when revival hit in Southern CA in the form of the "Jesus Movement" in the early '70's, I was ripe for picking. I was 19 years old and by some miracle had escaped drinking and drugs. I was raised as a good Catholic girl talented in art and writing. But my true desire was to be married and raise my own family. It would be my chance to raise a good family; a loving family, not the kind that I had grown up in.

I had an easy time in high school dating and having boy-friends and now that I was "saved," I was going to meet and marry a nice a Christian man and raise a nice Christian family. I was very naïve. I really thought that other people who said they were committed to Christ were as honest as me. I can't tell you how far from true that is. To make a long story short I met J— at an unaccredited Bible school. It was also an outreach to the community. He came right from high school. He and a close friend had been teaching bible studies in their home town all through high school and had come to the bible school at the recommendation of the pastor of church we all attended. It was an exciting time. God was moving and being a part of something bigger than me was important to me since I had grown up so unwanted, so rejected, and so empty. I realized for the first time that there was a purpose for my existence, and that God had a plan for my life. And I still believe that even though the script has been drastically altered. J--- has always said that within the first month of meeting me, he told his best friend, "I'm going to marry that girl." He befriended me; I really had no attraction to him. But as we started talking, I started to really admire him. He wasn't like any other guy I had ever known. For one thing, he was very self-controlled. Wow! I had never seen that before! I thought it was a very godly trait.

He was kind, funny, and smart. His vision was to be in the ministry. He was going to help his best friend start a church and then one day be the pastor of his own. He said he didn't have a problem lusting after women because all women were his sisters. I thought, "Wow, he's so godly-- it's amazing!" It made

100

me feel like I was privileged to know him! He was going some-where big! He was so holy!!! God was really going to use him.

For a long time I didn't know he liked me. Finally when I found out, I told my friends that he seemed more like a brother to me. However as time went on I really started to care about him. To me this was true love. I was going to marry my best friend. He had all the qualities I wanted in a husband and after two years of knowing him, when he asked me to marry him I said, "Yes!"

Now looking back there were a couple details that should have been red flags for me:

1. When we were alone he would go long periods without talk-ing, and when he did talk it was never about his feelings or what was going on inside him, he was emotionally unavail-able.
2. When his father had taken him to a whore house to have sex he told his father, "No, I can't do that. All women are my sisters." His father accused him of being gay. I found out later that was a clue to his real sexual orientation. The godly answer would have been, "I have dedicated my life to God, and for me that would be a sin."

The talking part I thought would change over time because when teaching a bible study and in groups in general, he talked all the time. And the accusation of his father was par for the course with his dad who was a violent alcoholic and not to be trusted. So on a beautiful day in July of 1977 I married my friend. I thought it was a brilliant union! Those first few years of marriage were like a little piece of heaven. Sex was good, we were helping his best friend from high school start a church, and it was growing over night by leaps and bounds. Both men were very gifted. Although his best friends wife thought of J--- as a threat, since they could communicate without even talking, all of sudden they were laughing because they knew what the other was thinking. Kind of creepy looking back, but then I thought, "So what, they have known each other for years."

Over a span of 17 years, we moved from California to Oregon, back to California and then Wisconsin where J--- was again an associate pastor on staff of a very large church. Those were happy years; however, as happy as I was and as amazing as I thought sex was, he seemed flat, never really happy, always in check, and always in control. If I ever brought these things up, he would say nothing. I didn't realize he was a troubled man with many secrets. I was exactly what he needed, a Godly wife to validate his ministry and make him look good.

By the time he felt he wanted to venture out on his own and be a senior pastor of his own church, we had five children. After much consideration and prayer it was decided that we would move to the mountains of Utah. So we lived a lot of life and one more child was born in Utah. We now had six wonderful children--the fourth being the only girl. By the time our youngest was four years old, our oldest had gotten married and made Grant an uncle!

Life seemed pretty normal, except sex was becoming almost non-existent, and   J--- seemed unhappy. I thought it had to do with our struggling church and burnout more than anything else. Plus we were getting older, so I thought his lack of interest in sex had something to do with age. When we did have sex, he struggled to keep an erection during sex, but he seemed fine if he was satisfied manually. I chalked it up to stress.

He had also developed a relationship with his computer that I couldn't understand, and I was starting to feel completely shut out of his life. I looked at him one day and said, "Are you living a double life?" He said nothing. I thought, "Nay, he's home to much to have a family somewhere else."

Our oldest finished His Master's Degree in Biblical Studies, and he and his wife wanted to move to Utah to help with the church. That was in 2001. By the fall of 2007, our daughter was off to college. Our next son was in high school and our youngest in sixth grade. J--- seemed more depressed than ever. I started meeting with two close friends to pray for us both but mainly for me as I was starting to feel so repulsed by him and angry. It's like my spirit knew before my mind did, and I was having a bodily reaction to J---. I knew something was wrong but could not get him to talk.

Finally in October, he decided to go on a sabbatical. Mind you all this time before the sabbatical he was still giving sermons, doing marriage ceremonies, funerals, and other pastoral duties. Finally I called Focus on the Families' Ministry Hot Line and described what I was seeing and told them how shut down he was. They suggested we go to their website and ask him to pick one of the many retreats they had available for pastors and wives. J--- did--he picked a counseling retreat. I thought, "Whew – finally we will get to the bottom of all this. He probably just wants out of the ministry."

It was scheduled for January. But on a Sunday in November with him doing absolutely nothing while on sabbatical except sleeping and being adversarial with me, I brought him some tea and said, "It's time to talk!" He said, "What are we doing tomorrow?" I said, "The usual, everything!" He said, "Okay, tomorrow after your home from the courier route, we will talk." I said great!

What happened next is so serial. It is almost four years later, and I still find it shocking: I came home and sat down and he proceeded to tell me the biggest concocted story I have ever heard. At the time though I thought it was truth. He said, "Over Labor Day Weekend on Saturday in September, I decided to go to the city and buy a cigar and go to the park and smoke it. Well, it was suddenly like I was in a trance, and I ended up at a park where you can meet up with men. And the whole time I was thinking, what am I doing here? And I got ready to leave when a man approached me and said, 'Hey – what do you got there? Let's see what you got.' So I followed him to the restrooms, and he said again, 'Let me see what you got there.' We were only going to masturbate together, and when I put my hands to my pants, he pulled out a badge and arrested me. The car was impounded, I had to show up for a court date, and since it was a first time arrest it was not made public. I have never done anything like that before; I promise you it was the first time I had ever been to the park." J--- proceeded to fall on his knees crying and cursing his dad as if his dad was accusing him of being gay caused all this, and then he begged me to forgive him. He admitted to viewing homosexual porn constantly the week before the arrest and before that quite often.

The rest of the day and weeks are a blur – what had just happened? What did it mean? Was I okay? I couldn't tell. I didn't know what to do or who to talk to; was I suppose to talk to anyone? And who? I couldn't think--I didn't want to think. Did this mean he had ended our marriage of 30 years? Just like that it was over? And just like that, I entered a hell I thought I would never get out of. Whew–it's powerful what someone else's behavior can do.

As soon as the pain of what happened started to register in my brain and body, which took some time, the anger set in! Oh my–I have never known that level of anger. The betrayal I felt was overwhelming and there was still more to come. We both entered counseling with separate counselors. I was experience-ing unimaginable grief. Sometime after all this came out, he had a dissociative memory of sexual abuse that had happened to him at 13years old in the naval hospital after his appendix had been removed. He said that is why he did what he did and now he needed me more than ever. The only problem was is that I felt blown up, like I had just barely survived a massive explosion that he had ignited himself and now he wanted my support? What, had he lost his mind? Did he have any idea what he had done? It was weird!

By the end of January, the church closed. What an added grief. People were told he had a moral indiscretion, so people thought it was about another woman. I wish. The next nine months in particular were absolute, unabbreviated hell. I felt nothing but pure pain, and I wanted him to be in as much pain as I was in. I verbally lashed out at him every time we were alone. I took his very expensive humidor and cigars and shredded it all with an axe in the back yard screaming obscenities at the top of my lungs.

I had never said more than an occasional "shit" my whole life! Then I threw our beautifully engraved Champaign glasses from our wedding on the cement and they shattered. When the "creep" came home I told him he had some messes to clean up, because now he was doing "everything" and I was doing nothing! It really is true, "Hell has no fury like a woman scorned." I hadn't just been scorned though, my whole life, everything I thought to be true, holy and sacred was gone; my role as a pastor's wife, leading women's ministries, and being proud of J---. All of that was over! The rug had been pulled out from under me. Nothing was left. The only thing I had which is the only thing I could cling to was my relationship with God and my close friends. I cried all the time. I needed a lot of time alone to talk to God and my counselor.

The counseling retreat we went to in January was excellent, but I was still in too much pain and shock, so it was not as effective as it could have been. J--- was blaming me for the most ridiculous things you could imagine and flat out lying, and I was having a hard time standing up for myself. Before we left there, one counselor told me that if he was a liar and manipulator we would not be able to make it. At that time I was not really considering the gay part since he was adamant that he was not gay and he wanted to be married. He said he had never had sex with a man but admitted he had been unfaithful, whatever that meant.

I had not allowed J--- to come near me since the day he told me what happened, and I decided to keep him at arm's length to see just who he really was. I decided I could no longer trust what he said and that I needed to watch what he actually did. I was hoping he would do the work he needed to do. I hoped he really did want me. And I wanted to believe him.

Over the months that followed some alarming observations surfaced:

1. He could not seem to tell the truth to save his life.
2. He would tell the person he was talking to whatever he thought they wanted to hear. So if he was talking to the kids, he would say whatever he needed to so they would be sympathetic to him which involved him being a victim. That was his new persona, VICTIM!! Everything he did was because of the abuse he would say.
3. He would say one thing to me and the opposite to the other person. He was continually throwing me under the bus with his lies to our counselors and the kids.
4. He was adamant with others that he was working so hard on himself and his marriage when in reality he was doing nothing.
5. He started to bully me, and I started to recognize that when my body started to shake it was my body telling me I was being manipulated. I was starting to trust myself.
6. I realize now how he had tried to isolate me from Godly friends by telling lies about them.
7. He would use any one he could to do his dirty work for him. He was never honest enough to say how he really felt or what he really thought.

I found out he was made to tell me what happened by our pastor friend in a nearby city. Apparently a police officer showed up at his church and said, "You better check up on your pastor in----- city, he was arrested." So the pastor met with J--- and asked him what was going on and had he told me? J—said no. J—was told if he didn't tell me by such and such a date that he was going to tell me himself.

At 6 months out from J---'s disclosure, I finally said, "Okay, you don't get from A to Z with nothing in between. Tell me the rest, and it better be everything!"

He proceeded to tell me that three years after moving here, he went to the city to a pornography store to look at gay porn when he met eyes with another man and followed him to Wendy's bathroom and supposedly watched him masturbate. I said you only watched! He swore that was it, and then he ran away. He admitted being tempted his whole life with homosexuality. That he had been in and out of gay porn for years and that he masturbated a lot. That he did some other kinky things while masturbating. It was over load for me. He also admitted to our grown up sons that he had come awfully close to gay sex but didn't do it.

When I heard that I thought, "Okay, that is an admission to me. Somewhere along the line he did it. I was sure, and I no longer believed it was just "one" time at the park. He had been there before, but how often I don't know. I just know it is very unlikely to go to the park once and you get arrested never having been there before. It was all a big fabricated lie. I have never grieved so deeply in my life. All of this was too much for me.

I'm not sure when that I was given Bonnie Kaye's website, but I asked to be put on her email list. Then I got the courage to ask her THE QUESTION, "Do you think he is gay? He says he's not." I will never forget this. Bonnie said, "Of course he's gay."

I started reading everything I could find trying to understand my husband. It all seemed so confusing! Each newsletter I got helped me sort things out. The most helpful information for me was learning the difference between a man's sexual orientation and his sexual identity. J—does not want to be gay and to this day says he's not. However, a person's sexual orientation, what turns them on, is what it is. Even Christian organizations admit that sexual orientation cannot be changed. They can only work with their identity and to help them and give them hope that they can live straight through hard work they renamed "homo-sexuality" as "same sex attraction." But they will always be tempted, and a woman will never really turn them on.

I finally understood why sex seemed like so much work to him and he couldn't keep an erection and he didn't seem to enjoy it. J—told me one day that there were whole studies done on the attraction men have to penises! Oh my God, I said, only if you're GAY!! I think us women have a very hard time understanding male sexuality.

For a long time I wanted to believe all J---'s lies. I didn't want our marriage to end. I no longer felt safe with all his lies and manipulation, but now when I told him I wanted him to leave, he refused and told me I should leave, that the boys wanted to live with him, so he should stay in the house. I thought fine, I can out last him.

I had joined a recovery group and turned on a dime, not reacting to him and keeping my boundaries while not expecting anything out of him. I was convinced he couldn't change, and he was incapable of doing the work he needed to do to be married. He was just doing whatever he could to make me be the one to file for divorce. So typical of his M O, letting others look like the bad guy. He never took responsibility for himself. He was completely immature displaying six year old behavior. That's all I ever saw.

By this time, we were in couple's therapy and it was a joke. The counselor was in way over her head. J—is a master liar! He is an absolute brilliant story teller! Everyone believes his crap except me which made him so angry! He got very passive aggressive. His anger seeped out sideways all over the place even to the point of purposely not talking to me as one of the ways he tried to provoke me. He was never even honest enough to admit when he was angry; his face would just contort, and he looked satanic. However, I was growing strong and becoming healthy and he couldn't control me anymore. It was feeling so good. I owned my power. I was becoming free. And God had my back.

I was now a year and half out from the trauma and I felt it was time to finally travel to see my parents and tell them EVERYTHING. I hadn't told them a thing because I thought if J—was going to "pull the ship up," why drag him through the dirt with my family? I started from the beginning. It took three hours to get through it all. At the end we were all crying. I sobbed on my dad's shoulder, he sobbed too. He said, "Honey, if we thought there was a way to fix this we would tell you to fix it. Some things can't be fixed. He came out, he's gay! Do you have a lawyer? Divorce him, I know you love him but there is no future with him. J-- ended it and this is his doing. He is responsible for what he did and the abuse is just an excuse, he made choices, he did this and he knew what he was doing. You can't fix this and all the counseling in the world will not help. It's over."

I asked my dad to pray for me, and he did, asking God to be with me and give me the strength to do what needed to be done. Up to this point I was still so conflicted. One part of me said this can't be over--we grew up together--we have six kids and four grandchildren. The other part of me was saying "I am so done! I can't do this anymore!"

Now everything was coming clear and it was time to act. My parents also said make sure to get AIDS tested and everything else. I did. It was so embarrassing, and then to be told you have no idea how many women come in here and test positive. Oh what a cruel, cruel thing to do to your wife who thinks you love her! How much more self- absorbed can a spouse be than that? I was very scared. It came back negative. I was clear. OMG, I got in my car a cried. Here we were on the cusp of heading into old age and this all felt like a cruel joke! The betrayal cut me so deep. The amount of deception was hideous on every level and never ended.

He lied the day he moved out of the house! There was no understanding from   J--- of what he had done to me. He acted heartless to me. The most he had ever said was, "I am sorry for what I put you through." What did that mean? Sorry for what I put you through? That was it? Absolutely no level of acknowledgement of what he had done. Only blame and more blame of what I had not done for him. It was hideous-- absolutely hideous. I was not the one who had exploded this marriage, and yet that is how he wants to portray me. I never claimed to be perfect, but I did my best to make him happy. I did too much and took too much.

It seems to me that my whole life with him was a waste. It was a sham: he stole my youth, used me up, and threw me away. That's how I feel. The only positive thing that came out of this marriage was my children. I thank God for them even though right now they believe everything their dad tells them. I don't try to change that. In time I believe they will see their dad for who he really is, a very sick person who for whatever reason he can't live in reality. I pity him. My dad says he broke his brain. I think he is right. I have worked very hard to put all this in God's hands and keep it there. Letting God be in control of outcomes has given me a lot of peace. We did divorce; ironically it was finalized in July of 2010, only six days after our anniversary date.

My walk with God has never been closer. He has been with me every step of the way. Was I ever tempting for me to blame God? No, I know better than that. I did go through a period of time wondering why I was here. All I know is that His ways are beyond my understanding and He has always assured me that I would be okay, that He was in this with me and that He was the One delivering me from a very bad situation. He has me and all of this mess in His very capable hands and I can trust Him. I can even say I am blessed, so many miracles have happened and I have been truly astounded by that. I am even starting to look forward to this new season of life! Who knows what is around the corner! I am okay, and I truly thought I would never be okay.

Lisa's Story

I always knew that the problems in my marriage were my fault. As an overweight child I was constantly reminded of how unacceptable I was by my parents, relatives, peers, and sisters. I grew up knowing that I was not sexually attractive and consequently unworthy of love.

Some of my first memories are around the disappointment of others about how I looked, I was constantly (it seemed) measured, weighed, judged, put on diets, and talked about. The main issue seemed to be that I would never find a man, and in my family that was considered to be the worst possible fate.

During my teenage years I knew deep down that I was unattractive, and I had little male attention which confirmed this belief. Where there was interest shown, I rebuffed the suitor almost subconsciously. There were also times when I put myself in danger by being totally unaware of a man's sexual interest in me. My only relationship prior to meeting my husband was very physical but disrespectful. This man wanted me sexually but did not want to introduce me to his friends or family. This confirmed my belief that I was not worthy of anything more; he was guilty about his attraction to me and ashamed to show me to anyone else.

So when Tim came along and gave me attention without making sexual demands, I fell in love quickly and completely. I was so besotted that I turned a blind eye to the fact that it was me who initiated our first kiss and first intimate moments. I was also not put off by his absolute determination that we should first and foremost be "best friends". I remember feeling so superior at a church run "Engaged Encounter" weekend. Couples were separated at night in an attempt to discourage pre-marriage intimacy. While all the other men were trying to negotiate room swaps in order to be near their partners, my finance was not at all concerned. I was so impressed by his restraint and maturity; "Those other men could learn a thing or two from him," I thought. His answers to the pre-marriage compatibility questions were textbook perfect, so the priest was sure we were going to have a great marriage. Tim also insisted that we should not have sex until we were married. It was a pity that the priest didn't think to ask husband to be if he was sexually attracted to men.

I remember my immense disappointment on our wedding night and honeymoon. Where was the grand, uncontrolled passion? The nights of endless intimacy? Certainly not in my marriage; something was missing. Deep down I knew it was because I was physically unattractive and unable to excite my husband. After just a few short months of marriage, our sex life was virtually non-existent and I knew why. I had put on weight and of course, that explained his lack of sexual interest. I found myself increasingly turning to food for comfort which resulted in further weight gain and even poorer self- esteem.

The birth of our first child and a move overseas away from family saw an escalation in our marriage problems. Our beautiful daughter became another excuse for avoiding intimacy; we were both so very tired and focused on her. A determined effort on my part resulted in a bit of physical contact and the conception of our second child, but as usual, it didn't last.

I was far away from all my supports, with young children, no job, and no friends while Tim was starting an exciting new phase in his career. I had given up a job with great prospects in order to follow him on his adventure, yet he didn't acknowledge my sacrifice and resented my need to have him home for company. I could feel the distance between us increasing, but I didn't know why. About this time, computers and access to the Internet were becoming more common. Tim started a phase of his research which required him to work alone overnight in a research lab with internet access. While I had no idea at the time, I now know that it was at this point, when our children were pre-schoolers, that he began visiting gay chat rooms and porn sites while working overnight.

I knew that something was wrong and that things were getting worse. I was fat and undesirable and now also depressed, withdrawn, and defeated. My husband kept saying that I was "blocking him out" and not talking to him. He was right. I didn't know what to say or what was wrong, but I knew that he never touched me nor did he love me the way I saw other men love their wives. I hid my sadness from the world, putting all my energy into my children and a new career. I dealt with my distress by doing the only thing I knew how to do--just keep going and smile on the outside. But I was sad and empty inside.

By the time we returned to Australia, I had reached crisis point. My husband had returned three months ahead of the children and me. He left me to sell the house and two cars, hold down a full time job and raise two young children by myself while he started his new job. I knew that other men did not do this type of thing to their wives, and that he just didn't love me in the same way as my sisters' partners loved them. Deep down I felt that this was all I deserved--that fat people didn't get to complain about the way someone treated them.

Shortly after I returned home, I was horrified to find evidence of Tim's online activity on our home computer. He dismissed my concerns by belittling me and telling me that I didn't understand how easy it was to get lost or misdirected while online. I was stunned and spent the next weeks in a daze. Up until this point, some eight years into our marriage, I had no idea that he had any interest in men. I insisted on marriage counseling, but was told by the counselor that this was all quite normal for heterosexual men and that I needed to be more accepting and open. Tim's response was that he just wanted me to forget about it and move on, as he had. I remember feeling absolutely bewildered but agreed that indeed I would try to be more open to such things and would try to be more communicative, as the marriage counselor was sure that my withdrawal was the cause of our problems. For a month or so there was a flurry of sexual activity but it all died off pretty quickly as I once again became tired of being the one to initiate intimacy.

I lived the next few years in a daze, functioning on the outside but completely broken inside. I was unable to express to my pain and was so ashamed that I withdrew from friends and family. I was unable to confide in anyone and consequently became more and more depressed. Finally I reached the point where I wanted to get healthy and take control of my life, subconsciously believing that if I could lose weight, my husband would be attracted to me. I joined a weight loss club and began exercising. I lost over 100 lbs. and the compliments came thick and fast from everyone, except from Tim who continued to ignore me. Our one attempt at intimacy was cut short when he complained that I was now "very bony." My self-esteem continued to plummet, and I struggled not to eat for comfort.

Over the next few years I developed a full blown eating disorder, binging, purging, starving, and over-exercising in an attempt to control my weight. Each night I would go to bed full of self-loathing at my inability to control myself and failure to attract my husband. Of course, I was always in bed alone as my husband had "lots of work to do" on the computer or would "fall asleep on the sofa" and not come to bed. Deep down I knew what he was up to, but I pushed it from my mind. I would lie in bed in fear of getting up lest I caught him in the act but unable to rest because I knew that it was me that had driven him to this.

Around this time he began to work late and on weekends. I was so overwhelmed with all that I was dealing with that I didn't even register the change in his habits. I sought the help of a psychologist who specialized in eating disorders. We did great work on my childhood issues, and I began to question my assumptions about my lack of attractiveness. I asked Tim to come to the sessions with me in order to talk through things that were stopping me from getting my eating disorders fully under control. In the first session he sat in the chair and told the psychologist that he "didn't know why I didn't realize that I could trust him, that he was a safe place for me to fall and that he was really distressed by the fact that I didn't allow myself to be vulnerable and share my innermost thoughts." Once again it was my fault, not because of my appearance this time but because I didn't trust him enough. He also said he didn't care how big or small I was--it did not alter how he felt about me (I now realize it was because I wasn't sexually attractive to him no matter what I looked like). As the psychologist started to delve more deeply, he suddenly "forgot' to come to a session, leaving me sitting there alone. No apology, he just "forgot" and I would just have to deal with it. He didn't attend again.

His night time computer antics continued as did my distress and self-loathing. I was so defeated that I didn't notice the increasing number of late meetings, weekend work, or the fact that he wouldn't let his phone out of his sight. Nor did I link these behaviors with the new underwear that he purchased, the fitness regime, and his desire to have treatment for his acne scarring. I was so lost and so busy hiding the shame of my failure as a wife that I didn't see what was in retrospect, so blindingly obvious.

One morning I awoke early, my husband was already awake "working" on the computer. When I walked into the living room he jumped up and pulled the plug of the computer out of the wall. That was a turning point; I had had enough and confronted him. He admitted that yes, he had been watching gay porn and visiting online chat sites for gay men throughout our marriage. I insisted that we go to a male marriage counselor. After hearing my story, the counselor insisted on seeing Tim alone. In the meantime Tim and I started talking and he begged for another chance. Wary of yet further deception, I directly asked him if he had ever been physically intimate with another man. He looked me in the eye and said "no". I agreed to try again and there was once again an attempt at intimacy. However, by this stage he could barely maintain an erection and did not climax. Once again I called my own desirability into question. His attempts to satisfy me through my clothes so that he did not have to touch me further crushed what little self-esteem I had left.

One morning, about a week after the attempted sex, I noticed small black "freckles" in my pubic region. Amazingly, I managed to put this to one side and go to work. That night, after my children were in bed I investigated further and discovered, to my horror, that I had pubic lice. In tears, but with more self-control and coldness than I had ever summonsed before, I confronted Tim, and told him that I had pubic lice. He initially denied that he had anything to do with this, mentioning that he too had been a "bit itchy down there" and looked at me blankly. This time I refused to be put off and kept questioning and demanding the truth, until finally the full story was revealed. Tim had, for a number of years, been hooking up with other men. Sometimes he would do beats, other times he would arrange to meet men through online chat sights. He had had sex in public toilets, in the beds of married men and in many other places. He had innumerable physical hookups, as well as regular online sexual activity.

To this day I am amazed at my inability to see what was so obvious. I also cannot believe that the man who promised to love and cherish me (and who still professes to love me) could have been intimate with me after putting his penis in so many other places and have put me in such physical and emotional danger.

Despite having only had intercourse with my husband, I had to endure the humiliation of having blood taken to test for AIDS and other sexually transmitted diseases and the various swabs that my doctor needed to take. While the medical professionals were very kind and comforted me as I sat there with the tears rolling down my face, my humiliation was complete.

In the following weeks I told very few people, I was so deeply ashamed and still felt responsible for what had happened. While I thought I was operating with a clear mind at the time, I wasn't. I was in survival mode, and I struggled to get through each day. I spent much of my private time in tears but maintained normal routines for the sake of my children.

As I started to come out of the fog, I realized that it was going to be some time before I could leave, but I knew that in time I would go. In order to have some sense of control while my world was in upheaval, I wrote a list of things I could do in order to get ready to leave. They included a plan for paying off credit cards, opening a savings account in my own name, starting to socialize independently, refusing to put up with any further deception and building my career so that I would in time, be able to obtain a promotion position in another state. I also took off my wedding ring.

I insisted that Tim tell the children that he was gay, but I ended up doing most of the comforting and explaining as he broke down after the initial "I'm gay." Their main concern was about what would happen to them, and it was for this reason that I chose to stay for another 18 months and keep our family intact until our youngest finished school. Today I live in another state and I do have that promotion position.

Our kids are now 18 and 20, and to this day, I have chosen not to burden them with the details of what happened in our marriage. They are lovely young people and Tim has been a great dad to them. I would not be without them and consequently do not wish I had never been married. Tim and I are friendly but only because I have decided that it is not healthy for me to hold a grudge. I will never fully recover from the emotional trauma of what he put me through nor understand how he could have knowingly put me at risk of sexually transmitted diseases. But as a consequence of what I have been through, I am a much stronger person and know that if I am still alive and kicking after the past 25 years of this marriage, there is nothing that I can't do. I am also much less emotionally reserved and able to discuss my feelings and I am slowly but surely gaining self- confidence. But there are still some very dark and lonely days, and it is hard to imagine that I will ever find someone to love me completely.

Interestingly my weight is not so much of an issue these days. I will never be thin but I no longer have an unhealthy relationship with food and find that I on most days, it is not such a struggle to stick to a sensible eating plan. As Bonnie says, Gay Husband Recovery does take time, but I am beginning to think that it is possible.

A couple of words of advice:

1. Give yourself permission to grieve; you have lost so much.
2. It is okay to take time to plan the best thing for you and your children.
3. Even though you may feel like you are okay in the early days, it is likely that you are not.
4. Take care in your decision making.
5. Some people feed on the misery of others (a couple of people befriended me because they wanted to be part of the drama and to know the gossip) be careful.
6. It is about him, not you.
7. No one deserves to be treated as we have been, regardless of how they look or what size they are.

Liz's Story

The Father, Son, and Unholy Ghost

A decade has passed since my separation and divorce from my college sweetheart. I am still confronted by friends and relatives; with expressions of disbelief about David's treatment, abuse, and lies. He was so good with an audience. He could be very charming.

The only person other than my children to witness his behavior was my sister. If not for her, many would have me believe I divorced the nicest man in the world. She lived with us during a very bad year of our marriage. Not the worst year; but a very, very bad year.

I am only now (mainly) over my marriage. It was 24 years of emotional abuse and sexual rejection. Both grew worse with each passing year. The emotional abuse became very bad when I was pregnant with our son. This was very confusing for me. I received no special treatment or kindness while pregnant, or while giving birth. I had trouble conceiving, and had required fertility drugs. I, and I thought my husband, were so happy that I was pregnant.

It took me a long time to get over my marriage. I doubted myself for years. My children took their Dad's side. They heard and saw their Dad yell, belittle, and threaten me for years. I physically put myself between both my son and daughter, and my husband several times, when he was raging at them. Most of the time, the rage fit was about a very minor incident.

He threw a very grand pity party. I was the one that left, so it was all my fault. He told his brother that he had no idea anything was wrong. I had moved to my own room, after once again he threatened to divorce me. He did this often during our sham of a marriage. This happened anytime I did not please him, and this was often.

The most damaging scene of my marriage happened during Christmas. We had two children, a 1 year old and a 3 year old. I do not remember having sex, but I was pregnant. He was not happy. He told me what a pain I was while pregnant. It was not a good time at his work. We did not have enough money. He did not want our daughter to be a middle child. He dropped me off at the abortion clinic and took the children to breakfast with Santa. I did not have the abortion. When he found out I was still pregnant, he went into a blind rage, calling me names and screaming that this was not what he wanted.

I had the abortion. He walked me to the clinic door. Such a gentleman. My Mother gave me a sexy black nightgown, stating maybe we would have another child. I have never liked Christmas since then.

I still blame myself for not having the courage to leave him. I know now that I have grieved for years about something I never had. I never had a marriage. I have also learned that grief can be felt physically. I mainly grieve now for my children. We were terrible role models for a loving marriage and family.

I could make this a real soap opera. My marriage had many sleazy moments. My children were the witness. To the outside world, he was such a nice man. He gave great gifts to me; especially in front of my family. I was silent about the verbal abuse and of our sexless marriage. I thought it was my fault when he told me at age 33 to consider us "companions." All that sex was just for movies and television marriages. He asked if I was starving. I was starving for some affection from my husband.

He became very successful in the oil industry. I stayed home with our children and did volunteer work. I went shopping. I never told anybody about our lack of physical affection. I did not tell any of the 5 different psychiatrists we saw during our marriage. I was too embarrassed.

I was a nice looking young woman. I worked out, took care of myself. I was always hoping he would notice me as a woman. I did not tell my best friends. I did not tell my family.

I envied my friends and their complaints of their husbands wanting sex all the time. I was allowed 1 or 2 sex acts per year. I felt like his sister and told him so. No response. Play like you do not hear. His usual answer to a question he did not want answered. I would always give up. If I did not give up, rage attacks would follow.

We never knew when he would come home primed to fight. He would criticize my family, friends, cooking, words, and character. I was blamed for his illness, his anger, his worries, the children's behavior, grades, health, noise etc.

He found a new friend right before the terrible Christmas. I was so happy he had a friend. They met every weekday morning at the club. I met this man and always knew he did not like me. We only went out once as couples, and it was not comfortable, and I did not understand why.

My husband told him very personal information, which was very unusual.

I was not allowed to tell my friends anything. I was silent. His rage was so great if I 'misspoke" or said anything he deemed inappropriate; I learned to keep my marital problems to myself. I did start a journal. I was reading my 10 year old journal right after I moved into my own room. I realized how unhealthy our marriage was when I came to an entry I had made, after his appointment with his psychiatrist.

He told me the doctor said his problem was similar to the man that had just been in. This man could not find sexual gratification without violence. It took me years to realize that my husband could not find sexual gratification with a woman.

I have found it most therapeutic to write in a journal. I wrote about things I was not allowed to speak about. Meanwhile I continued to exercise, go to the hairdresser, and do anything that would allow me some physical comfort from my husband. Nothing worked.

The most confusing part of our relationship was that at times we could have fun and be happy together. I just would never know who was coming home, Mr. Nice or Mr. Nasty. The longer the marriage, the more often Mr. Nasty arrived.

He was very homophobic. He did not want our son spending the night with friends. This would make him gay. He questioned how I had taught our daughter how to clean her female parts. He could smell her. She was a very young child, and a very clean little girl. He would bring home articles about menopause and throw them at me.

The biggest shock came 3 years after our divorce. He remarried, and both of my children were happy for their Dad. I called him to inquire why he was marrying again, as he did not like women. I remember his reply that they needed to marry soon, as vacations were planned and houses sold.

You might think of me as shallow and jealous, and yes I was. I was shocked and hurt. He, who had rejected me for years in our marriage bed, was remarrying. Bonnie's article about Straight Gay Men saved my sanity. I had out right asked him, before our separation, if he was gay. He would not answer. That was his way of answering anything, he did not wish to discuss. I could not imagine why he would want to be burdened with another female. It was such a dark day for me, his wedding day. I so questioned every thought and moment of our life together.

A few years ago, I told him, I had told our children that he was gay. His reply was that he did not think he was gay, as he did not fantasize about little boys. Both of my children have doubted me. Neither will discuss this with me. It is not a subject I enjoy discussing. They will not talk about him, just like he would not talk.

There were many red flags we both chose to ignore during courtship. I won't go into them. You would find me truly ignorant. That was truly my mental condition.

The past 4 years, our grown son has had so many problems. I have brought up being in the closet is such a sad place to hide. My ex refuses to discuss "it." He will not do it to help his son. I have no illusions that his truth would make our son's life all okay. It would help him accept who he is. Like Lady GaGa sings, "Born this way."

The Father part of the title is due to the emotional distance I have always known with my own Dad. It feels similar to the emotional distance I felt with my husband. We go back to the familiar. I did so on purpose. It felt like a normal relationship.

I have real trust issues with men. I have deliberately picked men to date that were inappropriate and not conclusive to a long lasting relationship. Yes, I am one messed up lady, and I have had lots of therapy. This last year I even saw a psychiatrist with his new wife. We did not discuss his sexuality. We were there to find answers for our son. My ex refused to attend, as he did not want to be analyzed. Like father, like son is a true statement.

I do not own a camera, nor do I like looking at old photographs. I can remember what was going on in my marriage, from the old pictures. I had not a clue as to the reasons for my husband's anger and belittling words. I realize now, that everything that I believed was a lie, that I spent years feeling bad about myself for being female. I want the twenty plus years back. I have accepted what is, but not the action that could lead to acceptance for my son's core being.

I heard the little voice, but paid no attention. I discounted my intuition, and allowed my husband to bully, manipulate, deceive, and abuse me. I placed no value in my worth, so why should he? Why should my children? I knew something was wrong, but assumed it was me. I was told so, over and over. Then it would be Christmas, or vacation time, or sometimes we were best friends.

I do understand how hard it was growing up in the 50's, confused about your sexuality. Denial. I have since learned that, the simplest explanation is usually the truth.

My old neighborhood had a lot of 50 year old married men "coming out of the closet." My ex is forever in the closet, I believe. I feel if he could accept himself as he is, it would allow our son to do the same. Maybe it would save a life.

123

The Unholy Ghost in the title refers to the lingering effects years of verbal and emotional abuse leave on the family. I still, at times, believe some of the things he made me feel about myself. The loss of confidence and sense of self, let alone self-esteem, that are the hallmark of living with a straight gay man. His ghost is everywhere. A lifetime is not left behind, no matter how painful.

I just want my son to know he is fine just as he is. There are other aspects of his life he needs to change. I want my daughter to have a happy, healthy respect for her role as a woman. I want her respect for me as her mother.

Ending my marriage was the hardest thing I have ever done. I left behind a life of privilege, friends, a home I loved, and my children's acceptance. I was the one that left and broke up our "happy" home.

Louisa's Story

I met my Gay Ex-Husband (GEH) in London through a mutual friend. We were both from other countries and we had a lot in common. We were both the eldest of six children, the same religion, very similar upbringings, and our birthdays were 3 days apart, though he was three years younger than me. His roommates were two girls, and his two best friends were girls though I knew he had not had many girlfriends. I had had plenty of boyfriends and had been in a long on/off relationship with a man who was Geographically Unsuitable (GU), given that we had never lived in the same country at the same time. I had been planning to meet him in New York but he kept postponing it, and when my GEH said that he wouldn't wait around if I were to go and meet Mr. GU, I felt that here was someone who wasn't afraid of a commitment so I went to NY with him instead. We continued dating, and he proposed while we were in USA, which was six months after we met. I was surprised by the sudden proposal and wanted time to think about it.

A few days after our return to London, I accepted. We had a long engagement to give our families time to organize a trip to the UK for the wedding (his from Australia, mine from The Netherlands), and in the meantime, we bought a small apartment and moved in together. He was always very attentive, much more romantic than me, and at times quite emotional. He worked in a small, male dominated office and didn't get on well with his boss, but got on much better with female colleagues than males. I never had any doubts about his fidelity to me – his female friends were just friends. Our sex life was fine, and for several years, we both worked hard, paid off some of the mortgage, and enjoyed our life in London.

The only major fly in the ointment was his boss. It got so bad at the first place that he changed jobs, ended up in a much larger organization but again, had a very poor relationship with the boss and changed jobs again. By this time, our first child had been born. He had always wanted a large family and was very pleased to be a dad. Like most new parents we struggled a bit, but he couldn't seem to relax with our son. He was very "Victorian" in his views and insisted on treating the child like a mini adult. He was very keen to show his son off, but not to get down to the nitty gritty work of child rearing, preferring to leave that to me. I returned to work, part time after six months. We moved to a different house closer to his work and mine, and this time he had a female boss who he got on extremely well with. That didn't last as she was transferred and it was back to a male boss who "hated" him.

Child number two was born, and I went back to work. We moved again so that he could change offices within the company and sure enough, he got another male boss who he didn't get on with. His parents were over from Australia on an extended trip and spent three months with us, going off on short journeys but coming back to us each time. By this time we had been together for ten years, and he had become a workaholic, leaving before 7a.m. and not coming home until mid or late evening. His parents often commented on his long work hours. He very rarely saw the children in the evenings, and spent the weekends gardening, at the gym, reading the papers, doing DIY, sleeping and generally unwinding.

There were times that I went looking for evidence of an affair, but I was looking for the wrong thing, and of course I never found lipstick or perfume or any trace of another female. At this stage I took the children and went to Australia for eight weeks, staying with his brother and wife who had three children of their own. During that time apart, he became very body-obsessed, spending long hours at the gym, and I now suspect, succumbing to the urge to explore the gay world. He met us in Australia for the last two weeks and we all went back to England.

I became pregnant with our third child, and he became more fixated on work. I had a hard pregnancy, and struggled to cope with two young children and an all-but-absent husband. Whenever I begged him to come home a bit earlier and help

126

out, his response was always "I'll try to be home early, but I know you can cope". He spent hours doing things for other people, but his own family came last. He was keen on taking the children to church each week and was happy to do anything which involved him taking them out for a while to show them off, and then returning to declare his exhaustion and need of a rest.

When our youngest was just a few months old, he started working at the main office, which was too far away to commute to, so he stayed there Monday through Thursday. When the local branch was to be closed and he was told, "Move or be unemployed," we decided to emigrate to Australia.

The next seven months were a flurry of activity: he away at work, me at home with three children, organizing the sale of the house, a move to the other side of the world and the 1001 things which needed to be arranged. The move was completed; we rented a house and he took temporary jobs whilst looking for a permanent one. After three months, he was offered a job 600 kilometers away (380 miles), in another state. I wasn't keen on this idea, as we had just moved across the world to be close to his family, leaving mine behind in Holland, and I felt that moving interstate was counterproductive to what we had both wanted. I told him then that if I had wanted to be a single parent, I would have been – but not like this. He insisted that he couldn't get a job in Brisbane, so we agreed that he would go for three months and if the job panned out, we would all move.

It did, so there I was again, with a house full of removal men, three young children and a husband nowhere to be seen. Within a few months, problems with the (male) boss started to appear, he was back to working until late in the evening, and I was despairing of ever having what I thought was a "normal" marriage. After almost 4 years of this, he was seconded to a branch in Sydney, so spent three months away from home again, returning every other week.

When he returned, things came to a head with his boss, and he wanted to move back to Brisbane. I put my foot down and said this was the last move – if he changed jobs again he had to commute as I wasn't going to go through the upheaval again, especially as our eldest child was due to start high school the next year. He asked for a transfer to Brisbane and started straight away, coming home every two or three weeks for the weekend. Our youngest had just started school and was having problems. I had started a part time job so once again I was juggling children, work, school, house sale etc with no husband and no relatives around. Four months later we were in Brisbane and he started going away again - five of the first six weeks after we moved involved him traveling interstate for work, and to meet up with one of the two girls who had been his best friends at school. The other one, incidentally, came out as a lesbian not long before this.

He started looking for another job in Brisbane, then applied for jobs in other states, one in the middle of nowhere, in a depressed area with few employment or educational prospects. Our relationship became quite strained – he was obviously going through some sort of crisis, but I was exhausted from 13 years of moving around, acting like a single parent and trying to work out what ailed our younger son. In the past, he had often told me how fantastic his communication skills were and that this always stood him in good stead in getting jobs, but he wouldn't communicate with me at that point–he just retreated into work. I refused to consider another move and told him that this was it–we were staying put and he had to either find a local job or lose his family. I tried to get him to see a doctor and made various suggestions, but he wouldn't consider any of them. We were renovating our house, which was very stressful. The renovations were finally completed, and we were able to settle back into a busy family life. Our youngest had by now been diagnosed with Tourettes and Aspergers Syndromes and he seemed to take this as a personal affront – he couldn't cope with a less than perfect child.

He had a female boss again, but he was spending long hours at work, and was very rarely home for dinner. This happened even when I fed the children first and waited for him to come home so that we could eat together, I ended up eating alone and he would put his in the microwave when he eventually got home. He was spending a lot of time at the gym, and his routine during the week was one of work/gym/late nights on the computer. On the weekends, he concentrated on the garden, the gym, and catching up on sleep. The children and I were a long way down on his priority list, and he never touched me or wanted sex.

Things came to a head when he joined a committee at our local church. He was able to get to their fortnightly early evening meetings, which then went on for a few hours, but was never able to get home to his family. When I suggested that he make the committee meeting evening a weekly routine so that he could alternate between the meeting and the children on the same day every week, he refused, citing "work pressure." I was becoming increasingly suspicious of an affair but again, there was no evidence of another woman. He always worked late one day a week so that he could collect our eldest child from choir rehearsal at 9 p.m., and on most other nights he stayed late because he said he needed to.

In mid May 2006, he was suddenly given a months notice with no reason. This was bizarre to me – he was the senior financial officer in a large organization, and it seemed to make no business sense to get rid of the CFO two weeks before the end of the financial year (June 30th in Australia). Three weeks later, a set of unusual circumstances led to my discovery of his old mobile phone with almost 100 text messages on it between him and his male lover. The penny finally dropped, although I was in shock and found it almost impossible to comprehend. The messages detailed a 3 month affair, begun on my 49th birthday, including a regular tryst on the nights when he was supposedly at work before collecting our son from choir. It was two more days before I was able to confront him about it. His reaction was "oh that's over" which I had gathered from the messages, but for me it was just starting.

It took some time to get (part of) the truth out of him. He had known in his teens that he was gay. He lived in a very conservative town then, and Australia in the late 1970s was not the place for a gay teen to come out. He spoke to his local priest about his urges, and says that the priest's reaction "scarred him for life." He never mentioned it again, to anyone, and after finishing college and working for a few years, he decided he would go traveling for a while and then join the priesthood. He met me during his travels, discarded the priest idea, and decided that marrying a baby incubator was a better idea.

After my discovery, he still wasn't ready to come out, and he wanted me to hide it and not tell anyone. I refused and told my sister and parents. He wanted to move into the spare room and have me pretend that everything was okay while giving him a chance to explore the gay scene from home. He was out of a job, so had plenty of time to do what he wanted, and he was in no hurry to look for another one. I wanted him to organize counseling for us together as a matter of urgency. Five weeks later we had one session, which was very emotional and didn't help me at all. We had another two sessions together but by this time he had joined three support groups for gay men/gay fathers. There was absolutely nothing available for me as a straight wife, and when I asked the gay dads group if they would put me in touch with some of the straight mums, their response was "that's not what we're here for". The sheer arrogance and selfishness of that group still takes my breath away. I wanted to talk to someone in the same boat as me, to get some idea on how to approach the subject with the children, not for a complaint session.

I did a lot of internet surfing on the topic and in the end felt that the children should know the truth. They knew something was wrong, were already upset, and I didn't want them to be in the dark. I insisted to GEH that we tell them and we agreed on a place, time and manner of doing it. He then told the two younger ones while I was out of the house for less than an hour one afternoon. It happened to be choir day for the oldest child so I told the GEH he had to tell him that day. He was 15, our daughter had just turned 13 and the youngest had turned 10 a week or so earlier. They all reacted differently. We then spoke to them together, with GEH explaining that he and I had been having some discussions and we had "discovered" that GEH was gay and he would be sleeping in the spare room for a little while. In an effort to keep my composure in front of them, I didn't remark on this outright lie, which is something I regretted later.

It took all my resources to keep myself from falling to pieces at this point. Antidepressants and counseling didn't really help. A regular routine and the support of close friends did. After five months of the GEH living in the house, going out late all dressed up, and coming home in the early hours of the morning, taking phone calls at all hours and disappearing into the garden to talk, I had had enough. He wasn't there for me as a husband or as a father to the children, and he was having his cake and eating it too.

I asked him to move out, at which point he said "I can't move out because you won't be able to cope." Since his mantra all through our marriage had been "I can't come home to help but I know you can cope," that statement got short shrift from me, and he moved out the next week. The next four years were all about his lifestyle, his needs, and everyone agreeing to what he wanted. I struggled with work, the day to day minutiae of single parenthood, being a straight wife who couldn't find any support, a GEH who came and went as he pleased, and his refusal to agree to a property split according to law. He wanted to split things down the middle, as by now he had huge lifestyle-related debts and needed money to pay them off. I held out for a better deal for the children and me, which I eventually got, after a protracted and costly legal battle. He earns four times what I do, and his earning capacity is much greater than mine, but he has been reluctant to pay child support (which by now is only for one child) and I ended up applying to a government agency which now collects it on my behalf.

I consider myself a strong person--educated, articulate and confident, but I was brought to my knees by the discovery of his homosexuality. Had he been honest afterwards, I might have been able to forgive his initial dishonesty, but he steadfastly maintains that he is the victim. He has always been controlling and manipulative in a charming way. He provided materially for us, but the emotional and mental cost of his deception has been almost too much to bear. The whole gamut of emotions has been like a never ending roller coaster ride, without any of the thrills. The initial discovery was like a tsunami, leaving devastation in its wake. Now that the debris has been cleared away, things look almost the same on the surface but the underlying structure has been weakened.

I have had a few dates, but each time discovered the man had lied about something critical, and I can't bring myself to trust a man again. If I do happen to meet someone and it works out, then fine, but I'm not looking. I am 54 and getting my life back on track is my goal for now. Friends, family, hobbies help give normality to my life, but I am very cynical and mistrustful of anyone new. I have absolutely no respect for GEH – I have to meet with him for the sake of the children, but if the day comes when I never have to speak to him again, that will be a happy day.

Maggie's Story

Lessons I Have Learned

If anyone had told me five years ago I'd be the ex-wife of a gay man, I'd have asked them if they were off their meds. What a preposterous idea, especially since my husband was from a conservative religious family – the proverbial "son of a preacher man." While he and I shared progressive views about homosexuality, his family didn't. They quoted Leviticus and Deuteronomy and shunned a member of the family who'd come out as gay. We both thought it was sad that they turned their back on this young man who'd found happiness with a same-sex partner and held a good job. How could they turn their backs on their own flesh? They'd never turned away the various nieces and nephews who'd run afoul of the law with drug problems, an arrest for theft and a couple of DUI charges.

But the Bible says homosexuality is an abomination and since that's what their father preached, that's what they believed. So how was my husband supposed to deal with the fact he was more attracted to men than women? He'd gotten into enough trouble for attending a high school dance. There was no way he could announce to the family that he was gay.

Prior to 1973, homosexuality was considered a mental disorder. But after studies revealed empirical evidence to the contrary and cultural views towards gays began to change, homosexuality was removed from the Diagnostic and Statistical Manual of Mental Disorders (DSM) classification of mental disorders in 1973. It was initially replaced by Sexual Orientation Disturbance, which was a compromise between homosexuality being a mental disorder and a normal sexual deviation. In 1986, it was removed from the DSM entirely.

Preachers from little country churches don't read the DSM, and even if they did, the Bible says homosexuality is a sin, and that's the end of the discussion as far as they are concerned.

Faced with that dilemma, my husband chose the route often "prescribed" for gay men: get married and that will "cure" it.

While he wasn't cured, for three decades he was able to suppress the urges by viewing gay pornographic magazines and when the internet came along, he was able to find material online. Then one December night when I was on an overnight trip with several girlfriends, he took the bold step of going to a local gay club where he hooked up with a man and brought him home.

He told me later that he felt both freedom and guilt – freedom to be the person he was meant to be and guilt that he had engaged in gay sex. Under the guise of seeking help for work and family-related stress, he sought psychological help about his confusion and was told by the psychologist that he didn't really appear to be gay and that he should just go home and have sex with me because that would "cure" his confusion.

To his credit, my husband had himself tested for sexually transmitted diseases and initiated sex with me one night four months after his club visit. It was a disaster. He wasn't able to sustain an erection, and he convinced me that he had erectile dysfunction that was not responding to any of the commonly prescribed medications. I was understanding and never pressured him for more sex because I didn't want him to feel ashamed over something he couldn't control.

Our sex life had never been great, at least as far as I was concerned. In over thirty years of marriage, I never once achieved an orgasm from intercourse. Instead, my husband would roll over and tell me it was okay with him to "finish yourself off."

As a result, I always thought there was something wrong with me – that I was flawed sexually somehow. Because sex resulted in nothing but a mess for me to clean up, I grew to dislike it. My husband refused to take any responsibility for birth control, so over the years I used almost every method of contraception available at that time. After two problem pregnancies that fortunately resulted in two healthy children, I did not want to risk another pregnancy. My husband would not have a vasectomy, so I again bore the responsibility of contraception, this time by having my tubes tied.

Meanwhile, we raised children, built my husband's career, traveled and looked like the average American family. My husband was vain, far more so than I. But after hearing other women complain about their husbands' slovenly habits, I thought I was just lucky to have one who cared about his appearance. The fact he had plastic surgery at age 35 and began having hair weaves a few years later didn't raise any red flags either. He just wanted to look good.

When we bought a new house and he wanted to be involved in the decorating, I didn't think anything about that either. Friends had complained that their husbands didn't seem to care about the house except for whether it had a big screen TV for sports.

We had activities we did together as a couple, but we also had activities we participated in separately. I thought having both was important to our marriage because it kept us together as a couple but also let us grow our individual strengths. I'd seen my mother-in-law fall apart when her husband died because her whole life was wrapped up in his life as a minister. When he died and she was no longer the preacher's wife, she had no identity. I didn't want that for myself, not did I want my husband to ever be without interests of his own.

I'd given my complete trust to this man. Just as he could trust me completely, I believed I could trust him. But one day I happened upon his email open to a series of messages between him and another man. The messages were very sexual in nature and I could tell from the tone of them they weren't locker room "trash talk" or any kind of joke.

I went into deep denial not only because the messages challenged everything I believed was true, but also because Christmas was just three days away and I needed to bury the ugliness so I could get through the holidays.

I became the Queen of Denial. I wrapped myself in a cloak of disbelief, put a big crown of astonishment on my head and carried a scepter, which was inscribed with, "Oh my gosh, no, this cannot possibly be what it looks like." I reigned this way for six weeks until my curiosity got the best of me and I began to search for more proof that my husband might indeed be gay.

In her book "Infidelity Sleuth," Julia Hartley Moore wrote, "If you have nothing to hide, you hide nothing." My life was an open book and I'd believed my husband's was too until I began to dig and learn that he'd been hiding his behavior from me for over four years. I learned he had accounts on several online gay dating sites and used them to find sex partners. He traveled often on business and had a "man in every port." He even had locals whom he would meet at motels or invite into our home when I was gone.

The man I'd trusted for all those years used our marital bed for gay sex.

Ms. Moore gave tips for things to search for and places to look. The backpack I never paid any attention to became a focus of my scrutiny, and inside I found condoms, lubricant, an enema syringe for anal cleansing and something called "poppers." This is sold in sex shops as vinyl cleaner or liquid incense, but is an inhaled nitrate that relaxes smooth muscle to allow for easier anal penetration. It also delivers a brief high. The pack also contained a bottle of pills prescribed for erectile dysfunction – the same pills he'd told me didn't work.

I found photos on his computer and on the gay dating sites that proved the pills worked wonders provided his partner had the proper anatomy.

The more I saw, the angrier I became. But one other emotion rose to the surface too – fear. I'd never worked outside the home, so how would I support myself if I asked for a divorce? And what about our families? What sort of embarrassment would this cause for our children and other family members? And what about his devout family who shunned homosexuals? I did console myself with one thought: our children were grown and out on their own, so there'd be no custody or child support issues.

Fear kept me quiet, and in the end, that fear probably helped me make wise decisions. Another thing I learned from Ms. Moore's book was to share the problem with someone else because it helps you stop accepting the lies. She also advised not telling your spouse anything until you had a plan of action.

When I am asked what is the most important thing a woman should do when she first discovers her husband is gay, I suggest these two actions: share the problem with a trusted friend and find a good attorney with whom you can form a plan of action before you confront your husband.

I actually shared with three good friends, and among them they convinced me to seek therapy, to open a checking account in my name and start putting money into it, to get tested for STDs and to be very careful where I kept the information I was gathering about my gay husband. I highly recommend a good flash drive because almost anything can be photographed, screen printed and pasted into a word processing document or scanned, and stored on a flash drive that can be easily and safely hidden away. Just be sure to erase your computer history, but hope your husband isn't smart enough to erase his.

Because I'd been advised that outing a gay man could lead to violence, my therapist, attorney and I devised a plan to confront my husband with a letter I'd have delivered to his hotel during his next business trip. This would put thousands of miles between us and protect us both. We could talk on the phone before his return. At my attorney's advice, the letter did not include any samples of the information I'd gathered because that would alert him to what I knew and allow him to start covering his tracks. The attorney's plan was to blindside him.

Not only did we blindside him, we blindsided his attorney as well because he violated the cardinal rule between an attorney and client: do not withhold any information. He'd told his attorney he was gay. He had not, however, informed her of his status as a serial adulterer and promiscuous whore.

Our divorce, which could have and should have been over in a few months, stretched out over eighteen months, and I have no doubt that at some point when he nears retirement age he will try to drag me back into court and have our settlement altered.

I had believed that once we agreed on a settlement the nightmare would be over. I'm not sure it ever will be. He remained in the house and I moved to an apartment since I couldn't afford the house he'd moved us into just a month after the gay club incident. I've since learned it's common for an adulterous husband – gay or straight – to move the family because the wife then becomes so involved in the move and all its aftermath that she has no time to pay attention to how many nights he "works late" or "goes bowling with the guys." She's in new surroundings and must spend all her time building a new nest.

So a little over four years after I'd moved into what I considered my "dream home," I packed up all I could use and moved out again. My now ex-husband has a partner who moved in part-time before I'd even finished unpacking in my new place. That man now resides full-time in the house. He sleeps in the four-poster bed I carefully picked out and cooks in the kitchen I decorated. He also gets to play nursemaid because my ex-husband contracted HIV during a drunken night of unsafe sex with a married man he picked up online shortly before I moved out of the house. He and his current partner had been engaging in unprotected sex because they thought since they'd both tested negative for HIV it would be safe.

Their reasoning was flawed because they never factored in the uninhibiting effects of tequila. The partner dodged the HIV bullet, but now he makes sure the ex takes his meds and accompanies him to his doctor's appointments so two sets of ears hear what he's supposed to do to stay alive. Because it had been four years since we'd last had sex and I'd been tested for STDs two months before I confronted my ex about his homosexual affairs, the health department was not required to advise me of his HIV status.

Just as he was careless about leaving his email open, leaving his backpack lying around, leaving names and numbers of men on the backs of envelopes, he thoughtlessly tossed away the carbon copy of the change to his HIPAA agreement from our doctor's office. The notice stated that his HIV status was only to be revealed to his male partner. Of course, I knew that meant he was HIV positive because why worry about your status being revealed if you're negative? He also left out a prescription receipt from the local pharmacy. When I Googled the name of the drug, I learned it has only one use: the treatment of HIV.

The nightmare indeed continues. And what's my response when people ask about my divorce? Oh, I forgot to mention that one stipulation of the settlement was that we are both under a nondisclosure agreement that prohibits either of us from revealing anything about the reasons for the breakdown of our marriage. I can't even talk to my own children, though my ex has come out to them. However, they don't know about the HIV and if they suspect he had affairs, they've said nothing to me.

At first I thought my children being adults would protect them from the negative effects of their parents' divorce. Now I'm not so sure. Their parents' marriage was the foundation of their lives, and that's crumbled away. I worry they may question their own relationships. And because they're male, I worry that they will question their own sexual orientation. I'd like to unequivocally say they are not gay, but you can see that my gaydar isn't the best in the world. I'd also like to think they could come to me with anything since we've always had a solid, trusting relationship, but I thought I had that with their father too. My gut tells me they're straight, but I do wonder how my unmarried son will deal with this if he ever decides to marry. It can't be easy to tell your fiancée, "Oh and by the way, not only are my parents divorced, but my dad is gay and has a boyfriend."

I'm breaking the nondisclosure agreement right now, but am doing so under an anonymous name because I believe my story can be helpful to other straight wives.

Music plays an important part in my life. I have songs I listen to because the lyrics are soothing or empowering. One favorite is "Lessons to be Learned" by Barbra Streisand. Google the lyrics to see how powerful they are.

Over the last two years since I discovered my ex-husband's secret, I've asked myself a lot of questions. I've wondered if I could have seen this any sooner, and I don't believe I could have. We tend to not see things we're not looking for, and we don't look for things that violate our trust and belief system. I've also never asked myself what I did to deserve this lot in life because I never did anything to deserve this. I trusted him implicitly and that trust was unbelievably betrayed.

One other question that has dogged me is "Why me?" I'm an ordinary woman of higher-than-average intelligence who grew up thinking she'd meet her Prince Charming and live happily ever after. For a long time, I believed I'd done just that, and then my prince turned into a monster and life changed forever.

I found Bonnie's website at about the same time I found a local divorce and grief recovery group. Between the two of them, I think I've found the answer to "Why me." And what is it, you ask?

If I'm to survive this ordeal and get myself out of the "circle of crazy" that therapist Misti Lynn Hall refers to so often, I have to go back to some of the lyrics of the song. I have to keep looking inside myself, keep believing and keep loving myself through it all.

I also believe in a higher power and I believe God has a plan for me – to share the lessons I've learned with other straight wives so they can understand they didn't do anything to deserve what's happened to them and hopefully be able to answer for themselves their own question of "Why me."

Marie's Story

My story begins in college where I was studying nursing at aged 18. There, I met Jack whose real ambition was to become a doctor, and we instantly clicked. Throughout the first year, we became the best of friends. It occurred to me that he might be gay, but as I started to fall in love with him and the feelings were reciprocated those thoughts just left my head. He wasn't the average straight guy-- no interest in sports and more into his clothes and appearance. But I just thought he was a bit different because he was an only child who came from a broken home and I loved him for who he was.

Initially we had a wonderful relationship; he was good looking, charismatic and charming to my friends and family. I realize what talented actors these men are. Over the first two years, everything felt perfect. We were passionate, had meals out, romantic holidays, and he treated me like a princess. And that was it, he had lured me in. I thought he was the one, and we talked about marriage, children, building our dream home, and all our hopes for the future. But each year that went on in our relationship, he became more manipulative and started putting me down about my weight or appearance. He would put his career first, his pastime second, which happened to be a first aid voluntary organization which portrayed him as a good standing pillar of the community, his friends came third (many of which were gay) and I was lucky if I came fourth in his hectic lifestyle. He would never sacrifice any of the above to spend time with me. At this point I had settled for him, perhaps unknown to him he had beaten me down emotionally and led me to believe that I didn't deserve anyone else or that I would end up being alone so would be better off with him.

As I had no other relationship to compare it to, I thought this was the norm, that passion and desire decreased as the years went on. When I confronted him about not spending time with me, he would twist it until I was made to feel like a needy, nagging girl. He was overly fond of oral sex being performed on him. I realize now he was probably fantasizing about a man.

After three years, I decided I wanted to go on a break from him. We were both working as nurses, but he convinced me I was inadequate at my job. He had put himself on a pedestal of a prospective medical student and would condescendingly tell me I'm not suitable for a career in the medical field. He had become very controlling and wouldn't let me go through with the break up. I was made to feel like I would regret my decision and after a week, I found myself back in the relationship. This should have been an opportunity for him to "come out" to me, but he didn't take it and we continued to have a relationship for another two years.

During these final two years, we both made career changes and returned to college on other sides of the country. I got offered a place in a teacher training college; he thought the childlike mentality of the course would be more suited to me as he labeled me "stupid" and a "simpleton." He had been accepted to study medicine and it had definitely overshadowed me. I only saw him on alternate weekends but realized that I didn't miss him that much and that I could hold my own. I made new friends, socialized, and started to figure out who I was. I was happy and when I met up with him, he would bring me back to the low self esteemed girl he wanted me to be. However, I still thought he was "the one" because despite everything, there were also good times and I thought I loved him.

Our five year anniversary arrived. I made an effort to get him the perfect present, traveling a long journey to get it and spending a lot of money too. I think I fitted into that category that many straight wives are in which is always trying to please him. If I buy him the perfect gift, bake nice food, be nice to his family and friends, he will love me more. But none of that can ever work because I am not a man, and he could never have loved me the way I loved him. It is unfortunate for women like us because we are straight and attracted to the physical form of a male. While they might love us as friends or companions, they are probably repulsed by our female bodies. We shouldn't have to try and please these men; a straight partner will love you regardless and want to touch you and caress you even if you're not feeling the most attractive that day. They will see a beautiful woman that they desire.

A week after the anniversary and having received no present from him, he decided he wanted to go on a break because we had gotten together very young and neither of us had been with other people. He hoped that in the future we would get back together to marry and have a life together. He would be a qualified doctor by then, and my family had money and land so I would fit the bill as "the doctor's wife." I was devastated but supported his decision and hoped we would finally get back together. I made excuses for him telling my friends that it was the right decision for both of us.

Two months later he requested to meet up with me in which he admitted he was bisexual (he had known since he was 14) and was now currently in a relationship with a mutual gay friend of ours. He tried to justify that this was not the reason he broke up with me, nor did he ever feel the need to tell me about his sexual orientation as it didn't affect his daily life or our relationship. He tried to explain that what happened after we broke up was not planned. But I since found out that he had gotten with the guy three weeks after the break up which makes me wonder if it was going on when we were still together. I'll never know the answers to these questions because when someone lies to you for so long, you question if any of it was real. No matter what he says to me anymore, I won't know what to believe. He warned me not to tell certain friends of ours as he wasn't officially "out" yet. Again I was loyal to him and allowed him to keep a certain level of control over me. I dealt with this news in silence and disbelief although as time went on, I realized I didn't owe him anything and told who I liked about his carrying on.

Looking back, I probably made it too easy for him. He was such a coward and didn't even have the courage to out himself to our friends. Sometimes I think I need to forgive him or it will eat me up inside forever, but I can only forgive him if he is sorry for what he did to me. There is an arrogance about him that he shouldn't have to explain himself to anyone including me and I think he's convinced himself that he didn't do anything wrong.

My fear is that when he qualifies as a doctor, he won't want the dirty little secret of having a boyfriend, he will probably prey on an innocent young lady to marry and give him the perfect family. I have not seen him since the day he came out as bisexual to me and my last email was to tell him to be honest if he was ever with another girl and tell her of his orientation. He thanked me for my advice and said it's something he might consider. I have had such a lucky escape and a huge sense of relief that we weren't married or shared a home but part of me fears he will do it all over again to some other unsuspecting victim.

Although it was good closure on the relationship as I was kind of hanging on to the idea of getting back together and now I would never take him back, I still feel ashamed, humiliated and as though I was used for five years for him to cover up who he really was. I thought I knew him so well and now he might as well be a stranger. I feel angry that I didn't suspect something because in hindsight there were signs. I am left with feelings of anger, bitterness and wondering did he ever love me. But at least I can forget about him.

After the break up, I felt so alone. I had no job, no money and was living with my parents. I don't know where I found the strength but it must have been in there somewhere. I got a job as a teacher and moved to a different part of the country. I moved in with three wonderful male housemates who made me laugh again, brought me out dancing, for drinks and generally looked after me during those vulnerable times. My girlfriends were and still are amazing, and six months down the line when I'd occasionally have a bad day, they didn't judge me or expect me to be fully over the damage he caused me. While they couldn't possibly understand the psychological damage that was done to me, they had all been through heartbreak of varying degrees and supported me fully.

Another important lesson I learned from this experience is to not be so stereotypical. I never had a problem with homosexuals until this and suddenly I became extremely homophobic. I still had gay and bisexual friends that were not hurting anyone but I took my anger out on them. I became very insensitive stating that I hated gays and bisexuals, that they couldn't be trusted and am the contributors for spreading diseases. I was quite nasty and really didn't want anything to do with the gay community or if there were gays on the TV, I would state that they made me feel sick and changed the channel. However I've now learnt that I was a victim of homophobia and shouldn't be contributing to it further. If it was more acceptable in today's society, Jack wouldn't have felt the need to cover up his identity; he obviously wasn't confident or comfortable in his own skin and in many ways was forced by society to live a lie and in the process hurt me. I stopped having so much anger towards my homosexual friends because after all, they didn't do anything to me and were just "guilty by association". If anything they were a great support and tried to help me understand why Jack felt the need to do what he did. I sometimes wonder if we never got together as a couple would he still be my best friend and to be honest he probably would. But he can never be a part of my life again.

After almost a year I am nearly there. I am a more mature, complex version of the girl I was. But the spark is back in me. I have gone on fantastic holidays and nights out with friends, I am enjoying single life and get plenty of attention from men however I am taking my time in selecting the right one and don't want to rush into anything serious just yet. I hope in time I will let down the barrier that surrounds me and has tainted my trust in men. One night I told my housemate that Jack had ruined my life. He said "he'll only ruin your life, if you let him". And he was right, at 25 my life is just beginning and that chapter in my life is over. It made me the strong person I am now, but does not define me.

Marina's Story

Robert and I first met our junior year in college. He sat with me at lunch, and in conversation, we discovered that we had both registered for the same computer class for the coming semester. He later told me that he knew he would marry me the day we met. Of course, I mistakenly took that as an affirmation of his immediate attraction to me. Years later I would come to the sad realization that he had handpicked me because he perceived me as a strong, intelligent, and independent woman, one he believed would be able to survive the ultimate betrayal of love and trust that would inevitably be mine and one could serve well to bear and raise his children without being needy.

It was no coincidence that coming from the strict Italian Catholic family I was raised in, it would be easy for him to keep me at arm's length. If I had been worldlier, I might have been tipped off when he immediately suggested that we refrain from any physical displays of emotion while at school so if we ever broke off it would not be "uncomfortable." I probably would have wondered why he was adamant that we not have sex until we married so it would be "special" and certainly would have been less apt to accept his postponement of intimacy on our wedding night and again on arrival at our honeymoon destination.

The sad fact of the matter is that none of these bizarre behaviors caused me alarm. My limited dating in high school and college and the repeated warnings of my mother that "good girls don't go all the way" left me virtually paralyzed when it came to matters of the flesh. Sex was not an important part of our marriage, and when we did engage in it, it was without passion or lust.

Of course, I had these romantic fantasies that it would one day be like a scene from the latest romance novel or Cosmopolitan article that I was reading. The reality was that it was something he gave in to once a month when I would remind him that my period was due and we had not been intimate since my last period.

While I may have been naïve when it came to the short-comings of our sex life, from the beginning I craved more affection and reassurance of his love for me. Once when I was pushing the topic of why he never held me or told me he loved me, he told me he had a "Madonna" complex with regards to me and could not see me as a sexual being. When I would press him to cuddle with me, he would tell me his mother never expressed or showed her love for him, yet loved him dearly so he did not see the necessity of demonstrating this emotion. He would tell me, "Hugging and kissing "is for phonies," Ironically, I would learn many years later that my entire married life and existence was a "phony" in the purest sense of the word.

Our first five years of marriage were dominated by always keeping busy either by seeing his family or doing work in our home. We would buy a house and fix it up and it was as if the minute the last paint brush stroked the wall, he would be ready to sell and move on. I often wondered at his inability to stop and smell the flowers and enjoy the fruit of our efforts. It was as if he wanted to keep both of our minds and bodies so busy that I would not have the strength or inclination to question his continued lack of attention and affection, and maybe he would not have a minute to think about how unnatural our union was to him.

These first years of domestic business were gradually replaced by a five-year period of difficult pregnancies and births. Our first child, a boy, died several days after birth. I was devastated, and for the first time in our marriage, it showed signs of weakness. I believe this angered him as he had no tolerance for any frailty on my part. He was harsh and mean spirited towards me, almost as if he blamed me for the death of our baby.

Later in a therapy session with him, after we were separated, he would tell me of a "pact" with God that he made when he was a child---one he claimed in which he promised his first born son in exchange for being able to live a "normal" life. I was sickened when I heard that and realized how mentally ill he was. We were blessed with three more children, all girls over the next few years. When I had my third daughter by c-section I remember him saying repeatedly to both myself and everyone else that he "would never put me through that again." I wondered what he meant because I certainly did not see having our child as something that he had "put me through" but rather as something we shared together as a manifestation of our love.

At this point, I did not realize that providing him with a "normal" family was the sole purpose of our union. For the next few years, I submerged myself into motherhood and for the most part, I think he was relieved that I was neither seeking attention emotionally nor physically at this time. He did berate about my weight gain and constantly criticized my eating habits and appearance which whittled away at my self- esteem. In the meantime, he discovered a passion for working out with weights, becoming obsessive about it. If we went on vacation, the first thing he would check out would be the hotel gym. Often they did not meet his standards and he would seek out a local gym and take a short term membership there.

At home, he started coming home late after going to the gym after work every day and I became resentful after having spent the day tending to our family. Most nights I ate dinner alone with the kids while he worked out until the gym would close. He also seemed to make very close relationships with other male club members who shared his exercise passion, and it seemed to me he would meet them and be "best friends" in a day. He invited one particular man into our home, and he would cook and serve dinner on those nights. It was as if he was trying to impress him. I felt a tinge of jealousy but reminded myself that it was not fair of me to deny him male companionship, especially in the estrogen dominated environment of our home.

He would go above and beyond normal behavior when it came to dealing with these men. For example, he offered for one to come live with us while he was in between apartments.

When I challenged him on this, he berated me and told me I was unkind and antisocial. In fact, he would tolerate no criticism when it came to anything related to the gym or his workout buddies and was always quick to point out that he was a good provider, a good father, and he "deserved this enjoyment- the only thing he did for himself."

Repeatedly he would describe how he wanted to work out in his basement when he was a kid and his brothers and parents thought it was odd and that he would never let anything keep him from his passion again. At this time in my life, I felt that something was wrong but could not put a finger on it. For some reason, out of the blue one night, he told me he had a confession. Of course, I immediately assumed it was another woman and that explained his lack of attention to me. He explained that he had a problem with masturbation since he was a young boy and that he would masturbate several times a day and that was what was accounting for his lack of desire to be with me. He had come to a point in his life where he felt that he was cheating me of what I deserved He said he often needed three days notice in order to have sex with me in order to build up his ability to perform. Honestly, I was so relieved he wasn't having an affair I was almost thankful. He promised he would try to stop but warned me that he might need to have sex in the middle of the night, and that if that happened, he would have to wake me up and have sex to avoid masturbating. I was excited at the thought of having unplanned, spontaneous sex and dutifully told him I would stand by ready for duty. The first few nights, I primped myself before bed and wore a sexy nightgown as opposed to my normal flannel pajamas. After a week I asked him when he would wake me up. He laughed and pretended he hadn't said it. I asked him every few months over the next 15 or so years if he still had the masturbation problem, and his response was always that he had it under control. We never had that late night love making session.

When my youngest entered kindergarten, I felt I needed to get back to work full time to fill the void in my life which I still could not identify, but I knew was there. He encouraged me to go into the same business he was in--insurance. In fact, he conveniently suggested I go work for him and not return to accounting which I had my degree in. He reasoned this would give us the flexibility of having one of us around for the kids.

I never assumed that the one who would be taking time out for the kids would be anyone but me, but I was mistaken. Once I went to work with him, he capitalized on it and made sure he left early enough to go home and cook dinner for us—of course, after swinging by the gym for a few hours. He was now getting in a morning workout and an afternoon workout and his body had changed dramatically. He had developed his muscles to the point where he looked like he might be a body builder. All the while, I actually enjoyed working and didn't question his intentions.

After Sept 11, 2001, he suggested that it was best he be home more for the kids as they were getting older and needed someone to be around to keep an eye on them. Shaken by the events that had happened to our country, I agreed and he started coming to the office even less. Around this time, my oldest daughter was in high school, and he chaperoned an overnight trip for her class. When he came home, he talked incessantly about one of her classmates in his group and how he had spoken to him about working out. "Joey" was on the football team but really wanted to find out how Robert had gotten so "buff," and so began the beginning of my world spinning out of control.

Robert told me he wanted to train Joey. He went out and spent about $45,000 on exercise equipment to put in our basement, and he belonged to at least three gyms. He started having Joey come over every day to work out for two hours and then he would prepare a nutritious protein based meal for our family and Joey. I thought this was extremely strange and told him I was not comfortable with having this kid in the house every day. It was uncomfortable to get home from work and always have Joey around. Our potential liability if he accidentally injured the kid also was on my mind but Robert would hear nothing about it. He verbally cut me to pieces as was preferred approach using the, "You are not nice, and you are antisocial" attack, and would get his way.

We spent the summer of 2006 at a beach community about an hour from where we live. Packing to get ready for our trip, I went in his closet and opened a drawer and found a box of condoms which were most definitely not the brand or type that we used. I questioned him about it, and his response was that they were probably our daughters and she was hiding them. I question my state of mind in that I was so brain washed I was willing to accept the sheer absurdity of my daughter hiding latex condoms in of all places---her father's closet. Really? How much in denial was I that something was decidedly wrong in my marriage?

Our oldest daughter was now in college while her sisters were in high school. She capitalized on the party scene at the vacation home that summer and often would come home at night with her friends. I feared she was getting out of control and hoped he would step in and set some boundaries as the man of the house. Since he had never acted like a man up to this point, I do not know why I would expect that he would now. I remember lying in bed one night and hearing her come in with what sounded like an army at 2:00 a.m. I asked Rob to go upstairs and tell her friends that they had to go home. An hour later, when he had not returned to bed, I quickly dressed and slipped upstairs to find him cooking steaks at the grill with about six teenage guys surrounding him, intently listening to his advice on exercising. I was sickened but didn't rain on his parade.

When I questioned him about it the next day, he attacked me, calling me a party pooper. He knew my weaknesses and took aim right at them. Later that summer, I stepped on something in my bathroom that pinched me. Looking down I found a hypodermic needle. I was frightened and immediately went to his closet to see what I could find. Hidden in the pockets of his suit jackets were about a dozen different vials. I suspected they were steroids but wrote down the names and Googled them later that day. My suspicions were confirmed. I confronted Robert who talked his way out of it, claiming they were testosterone hormones the doctor gave him because his level was low. He claimed he was doing this for us so he would have more of a sex drive. I almost wanted to believe him but this time I knew better.

Frantic to get to the bottom of where he was getting the drugs, I told him I was staying home from work the next day to take care of a few things and that he would have to go in. He hadn't been to the office in a while and begrudgingly went. I was intent on finding out who was selling him these illegal drugs. I reasoned I would expose a whole steroid trafficking ring, and I would be on the news being interviewed. I needed to get on his computer but he had more passwords and locks on it than I could ever figure out. He always said it was because he had our banking records on there.

Frustrated, I called him and said I needed the passwords to get on because I needed to print something and the printer wasn't working with my computer. He gave me the passwords without questioning me further, and I set out on my detective work. I searched all his documents for receipts and found one or two, but not what I was really looking for. I was just about to give up when I saw a folder on his desktop that merely said "John." I immediately assumed that John was his drug dealer and opened the documents in the folder one by one.

At first, I didn't comprehend what I was reading. They seemed like short stories and the theme was always related to being at the gym. As I continued to read, I realized that the men in these stories were having sexual relations. I gasped for air, shocked, and not believing that I was reading male pornography stories. I started searching deeper into his hidden files and found sites he had visited. Many had sexually explicit names referring to male body parts in them. Still disbelieving, the final nail in the coffin was a downloaded porn flick. It was self-explanatory.

I reached for the phone and called him and said I needed him to come home to talk. He never asked why. An hour later, when he walked in the door, I demanded he explain why there was male porn on his computer. I am not sure what explanation I was hoping he would give me. To my surprise, he answered quickly and without hesitation those two words that would forever change my life, "I'm gay." At that point, the floor opened up and swallowed me. I did not know how to react. Disbelief, disgust, anger, and sorrow were all swelling inside of me. The first thing I probably said to him was, "What do you mean you're gay? You have been married to me for twenty-four years, we have three children, and we have a business together. How can this be?"

Then the remorse began and he backtracked and said that well maybe he was bisexual or just curious. Had he ever cheated on me? Of course not! It was something he had wrestled with and fought his whole life, but he would never act on it. He explained that he just watched male porn and masturbated to it, but that he had put that part of him in a compartment of his life that he never opened and he led his heterosexual life with me.

I stupidly wanted to believe that just like I wanted to believe that waiting to have sex with me was to make it "special," that only phonies showed affection, that my daughter hid her condoms in her father's closet, and that he was taking steroids so his testosterone levels would come up for our sex life. For me, accepting that he was bisexual, although devastating, was a lot easier to swallow.

I immediately recovered and went into "fixit" mode. I thought we would get through this, that we'd get help professionally and conquer it. He agreed that it was something we could work on. I feverishly searched the internet doing searches on wives of married men who thought they were gay. There seemed to be two schools of thought. Some said they loved their husbands and stayed in their marriages and worked at it. Of those, some claimed their husbands didn't act on it and some accepted their husbands outside activities as a small price to pay for salvaging their marriages. Many truly believed that their husbands could be attracted to both them and men. This was the camp I wanted to belong to and I was determined to find a therapist who would agree with me.

The other school of thought said that if your husband wants to be with a man, he is gay and you should get out of your marriage because you will never have what you want and desire from a man who is gay. I did not like this closed minded thinking and would automatically close those websites because they made me feel very uncomfortable.

Over the next month, we saw about four different therapists and a sex therapist. Deep inside, I thought there would be a pill I could give him to make him straight. If I didn't like the therapist, for example, if they told me that in most cases there is no way to work out this situation and stay in the marriage, I would stop going to them and find a new one. The one thing I did learn in all these sessions was that Rob had a sex addiction to male pornography and masturbation, and he was addicted to steroids fueled by extreme body dysmorphia (kind of the opposite of bulimia, he never thought he was built enough).

Of course, I was convinced that he must have been sexually abused by a male relative when he was a child, which would account for his attraction to men. He had no recollection of this but throughout the therapy, maintained that he had never acted on his desires. To fix things, I booked a romantic vacation to a couples resort in Mexico. Our sex therapist thought it was a good idea but warned us not to be intimate. That was not really an option as I for one had no sex drive at this point.

Before we left I ordered the book Straight Wives Shattered Lives. I knew nothing about it but hoped it might be helpful. That week in Mexico was a waste of time but for one thing. I read that book cover to cover and slowly came to the realization that there is no gray area. I was married to a gay man and that goes against the laws of nature. I owed it to myself to close this chapter of my life and get the love I deserved.

Things slowly became clearer to me, and I saw the web of lies and deceit Rob had woven for over 24 years. I did not like seeing this and had moments where I regressed. In a moment of weakness and desperation, I researched sex addiction rehab facilities and found an acclaimed facility in Arizona. I used our life savings to book him there for a six-week treatment program with the hope that he would reconcile some horrible childhood event that drove him to his love and desire of men. He gave me no fight on this –probably the first thing he didn't challenge. He dutifully boarded the airplane I had booked and never asked me a thing about where he was going.

I secretly hoped they could fix him and let him see how wrong he was, but I knew that I was grasping at straws. I dragged my three daughters there to visit him for family week where we would sit in therapy with him and his group, and they were to take responsibility for their addiction and apologize to their family for the harm they caused. After three days, his counselor told me not to bother coming back—he was not showing accountability for his actions and the hurt he had caused us. The staff did not think he was ready to go back into his normal life and recommended him to another sexual addiction treatment facility for three weeks of after care.

While he was gone, I discovered evidence that he had been with one of his gym friends and slept in my bed with him. I came to the realization that his claim that he had never acted on his thoughts was just another one of his lies, and I told him he could not move back in with us after rehab. His parents and family were sympathetic to him and probably wanted to believe I was accusing him falsely.

In one final attempt to convince my daughters and his family of the truth, I hired a private detective to trail him when he flew home from rehab, and of course, this confirmed that he was having a relationship with a man. I knew then and there that I could not be with him and told him I would file for divorce.

It has been almost five year since that fateful day when I found porn on his computer. Despite him maintaining that he was bisexual after he returned from rehab and against his counselor's recommendation, he immediately began dating men and moved in with someone. He has been in that relationship for three years. I still work with him and it is a difficult thing for me to see him every day.

Our children have met his boyfriend and have been forced to deal with the situation. They are bitter and resentful and blame me for what happened. They cannot blame him because they are neither certain of his love nor will he tolerate any criticism from them or anyone else. He has made himself out to be the martyr in all of this and will tell anyone who will listen of the suffering he endured in denying who he was all those years.

I have no sympathy for him and see him as a coward who used me to shield himself from a world that might not have embraced him. He has never expressed any regret for what he did and maintains that it was never his intention to come out but he could no longer live that way.

At this time, I see him for the liar he was and still is. As he once told me in therapy that he grew up lying since he realized he was attracted to men at age five, and he became a master at it, fooling his family, close friends, and ultimately me and our daughters. He was "on" 24 hours a day and never once let down his guard until eventually it became too difficult to hide with his addictions making him sloppy. It is part of who he is and comes naturally.

Since I work with him, I know he lies to me on a daily basis, but the difference is that now I can see through the deceit and no longer make excuses for him. His narcissism is stronger than ever. We recently attended my daughter's graduation and he was quick to point out to me how many men were "checking him out." He even suggested that I accompany him to a gay bar so that I see myself how many of the men there are married or in heterosexual relationships. I did not accept his generous offer, but it is hurtful to think of the men out there still deceiving their families.

As for me, I finally have found the guy in the Cosmopolitan article from 30 years ago. I now know what it feels like to have someone adore you for who you are and look at you like you are the most beautiful woman in the world. It feels wonderful to be desired by a man and I am enjoying being spoiled by someone who opens the door for me instead of the other way around. Life for me began at 47, and I am learning new things about myself every day including learning to stop and smell the flowers. Although I took the path that was much more difficult for me, I have no regrets of the decision I made to move on and the example I set for my daughters in never settling for less than what you deserve.

Mary's Story

I first met my husband in 2004 and it was on Halloween. We were both at a mutual friend's house and were introduced to each other. He asked me if I wanted to see a movie later on, and I said no due to the fact I was 50 and he was 29. I really didn't feel we had a lot in common. HE asked me again, and I said okay. I figured what can it hurt? I had no plans that evening.

After that he asked me out for dinner and we started dating afterwards. Even though there was a significant age difference between us, we both enjoyed eating out, movies, and baseball. He was a very mature 29 years old. He didn't have a religious background, and I was raised Baptist. Of course, my religion believed being gay or lesbian was a sin.

After a year of living together, I really fell in love with him. I asked him to marry me, but he turned down my offer saying that he wasn't ready for that kind of relationship. I had been married before and divorced, and he was married before and divorced. We continued to date, and after another year, he asked me to marry him and I said yes. We were married and very happy and our sex life was really good at that point. He was the most kind and generous man I had been with in a long time. He sent me flowers for no reason, bought me gifts for no reason, and never once did he forget our anniversary or my birthday. He was such a romantic at times that I couldn't believe it--I truly felt like a queen.

After being married a year, we moved to a place called Wilton Manors which I did not know was 40% gay. I guess that was the first red flag I missed. My husband quickly became involved in the community and became president of the board of the committee where we lived. Most all the other board members were gay. I still felt no threat at that time since most of them had their own partners. I thought they were really nice, and we had board meetings in our home and went to dinner with the board members many times.

One of the board members, the vice president, was gay, but he didn't have a partner. My husband and he spent a lot of time together planning events for the community and fund raisers. During this time my husband still was attentive to me but not as much as before. I began to feel a detachment, but I thought I was over reacting. I told myself that he was just really busy, and it was just me but stills something didn't feel right. At that point, I probably had missed several red flags because I am a very trusting person and also very passive.

A year later my husband came to me one night and told me he thought he may be gay. I know this will sound strange, but you could have knocked me over with a feather. I asked him where that was coming from, and he said he had always been attracted to boys instead of girls from even when he was a little boy. He told me that he had feelings for the vice president that he had spent a lot of time with and he was attracted to him sexually.

I became very angry and asked him why he married me if he felt this way, and all he could say was he never meant to hurt me. I told him this was unacceptable and that he needed to move out. I felt so used and so hurt that he had deceived me in this way, and I never felt so alone in my entire life. My children were grown and one lived up north and the other lived in another part of Ft. Lauderdale at the time, so had no one to talk to. I was also too ashamed to let my children know what had happened. All I could do was cry and try to figure out what to do next.

Strange at is may seem, I went to a totally gay bar one night to try to find some answers. I am not sure what kind of answers I thought I was going to find at a gay bar, and I left feeling worse than ever. I felt like my life was so out of control, and I couldn't fix it or put it back together. I went to sleep crying and went to work crying and came home crying. To this day, four and one half years later, I still have crying episodes.

My husband came to me a week later after coming out as gay with two dozen roses and said he wanted to stay in the marriage because he did not want to hurt me like he had done. I told him it was too late and we needed to move on and get a divorce. He agreed to file for a divorce so I wouldn't have to and agreed to pay me alimony for the five years we were together. He also gave me all of our savings and paid my bills until I moved to another community in Ft. Lauderdale.

My ex-husband's story continues to get more interesting with time. After living with his partner for two years, they split up because my ex wanted to express himself by dressing in women's clothing wearing makeup and jewelry and his partner wanted no part of that. I truly feel like my ex is having some sort of gender crisis but that is no longer my problem. I hope one day he finds what he is searching for. We are still friends and have lunch every now and then. I also want to add that he has never missed an alimony payment in four years, and continues to tell me that his only regret is that he could not keep his commitment to our marriage.

It wasn't until I found Bonnie Kaye's support group that I could begin to start to heal. I still haven't started dating again because I am still trying to get my trust back and every man I look at I automatically and I do mean automatically wonder what they are hiding. I am learning to love myself again and I am learning not to rely on anyone else for my happiness.

I would like to say in closing that I fully understand what Bonnie means when she says our husbands love us to the degree that they can love us when they are with us. I remember one night after me and my ex had been together for about two years he turned to me and said that I didn't deserve him--I deserved so much better. It didn't mean too much to me at the time, but it sure is as plain as day to me now.

For all of you ladies, if you ever need to talk or just have someone to listen, I am always there and you may get my email from Bonnie. I thank god for Bonnie and her support group. She was with me every step of the way, and I will never forget that. Remember ladies if you ever lose your husband to a man or a woman, it makes no difference which one--you never really had him to begin with. So always trust your instincts and never take anything for granted. This means you should always question anything that doesn't feel right. God Bless each and every one of you for your strength and courage.

Molly's Story

We met through mutual friends at the age of 20. Joe was handsome, funny, and athletic and had a good job with his family owned business. He had just ended a one year relationship with a girl from work. I was working full-time, attending college part time, and living in a chaotic household with my on-again/off-again divorcing parents and two younger sisters.

Joe lived at home with his crazy-in-love parents, two grandfathers, sister and a menagerie of pets. Our mutual attraction was evident from the first meeting and I knew he was "the one". He was a gentleman. I never had to push him away from me because things were progressing too quickly. He told me that he and his ex-girlfriend had done everything but..... and that he was still a virgin (at age 20). I felt awful that I could not say those same words to him. After five months of dating, "it" finally happened! Then, four months later, after knowing each other for nine months, he bought me a ring and asked me to marry him.

We had a year-long engagement and as the wedding day neared, we both questioned whether or not we were ready for this. We decided to go for it but would hold off starting a family until we were sure this was going to work. Looking back, our wedding night should have been the first clue but I was too blind to see it and the thought never even crossed my mind! After the party we had gone back to our apartment to spend our first night together as Mr. and Mrs. We were leaving early in the morning for our honeymoon and he mentioned that he was tired and needed sleep. Oh no!

I thought sex would have been a bigger part of our marriage. I'm not saying our sex life was completely non-existent--it was just "there". Just after our second anniversary, our first child was born followed by two more within the next three years. I had everything I ever wanted: a husband and family. Life was good! Since I was not employed outside the home, I threw myself into raising our family while he worked, worked, worked. To advance in his career, he was offered a move out of state and after must protest, I agreed to go. He really wanted this. Good wives do this for their husbands, right?

He worked long hours while I stayed at home with three babies. That's when I began finding receipts from restaurants and movie ticket stubs in his pockets. The object of his affection was a woman from work. I don't believe he had a sexual relationship with her but he was spending time with her taking time away from the kids and me. He then announced that he needed something more than me and the kids. This was the second red flag that our marriage was in trouble.

Fast forward 12 years: I started feeling as if something was wrong and I knew I wanted out of the marriage. I had no concrete reason; I just knew I was miserable when I was around him. He was not outwardly cruel to me, but his passive/aggressive behavior was driving me away. At this point, our sex life was non-existent. We were roommates and parents.

When I finally got up enough nerve to tell my family (parents and sisters), they were all upset (except for my father) that my kids would be from a broken-home and I felt they blamed me for my unhappiness. Was I perhaps going through early menopause? Did I need to take a trip by myself? Maybe the whole marriage and family life was getting to me. Everyone had advice. At this point, I had gone back to work full-time after being a stay-at-home mom for 17 years. I loved my job, the people, and the time away from 'him.' I was so happy at work but the minute I walked back into the house, I was miserable again. I rented an apartment in our small town and moved out. We had a shared custody arrangement which worked out well.

Five months after I moved out, I stopped at the house to pick up the kids when he announced he had met a woman on a dating website and he was going to start dating. This hit me like a ton of bricks. How dare he? For whatever reason, I decided I wanted him back in the worst way. He was open to it and we began to date. We (or at least I) fell in love all over again and started marriage counseling to give this time our all; it was one last shot at keeping our family together.

He seemed thrilled that I was back, and I was thrilled to be back. I kept my apartment while he stayed in the house, but we would meet at restaurants, movie theater, coffee shops or have dinner at each other's homes. The sex had never been this good! My heart was happy again and I was in love with the man I had married 22 years ago. Life was good--no great--again!

I moved back into the house two months later. The day after (literally) my furniture was moved back into the home is when sh__ hit the fan. We were trying to find a good home for our pet rabbit. Someone suggested I put an ad on Craigslist. I had heard of it but had never been on the site. I logged on, typed in my ad then decided to click around since I was not familiar with Craigslist. Curiosity got the best of me and I clicked on "personals"....then on M4M.

What's that? OH! I typed in our hometown and saw all kinds of crazy ads/photos for M4M. Men were trying to hook up with other men for blow jobs in cars, their homes, in parks, anywhere/anytime!! I have to admit, I thought it was funny but also sad at the same time. It was sad because some men admitted to being married in their ads. Why in the world would a married man need to post an ad like this or better yet, why would he be seeking out another male for a blowjob? I mentioned this to Joe as I was leaving for work that morning.

After work, I had gone back to my apartment to grab some last minute things I had not packed. One thing was my computer. I logged on to read my email when all of a sudden a little box popped up "you've got mail". Huh? I had not seen this message for years and had completely forgotten about an old email account that our entire family shared way back when. I logged onto our old account and saw, yes, we did have mail. Boy, did we have mail.

The third red flag that our marriage was about to be blown to pieces appeared. As I read an email trail that started shortly after I left for work, my heart felt as if it would thump out of my chest. My first thought was "oh my God, someone got a hold of our email password and they are playing a joke on us." As I read the email that was obviously between two men who had hooked up on Craigslist earlier in the day and were planning their meeting while talking about what they were going to do to each other, I realized my life was going to change at that very moment. When the man my husband was chatting with asked him to send a photo, he sent it. He sent a very nice one of him all suntanned on a beach in the Bahamas. I hadn't seen the photo in years. He even cropped our youngest daughter out of the picture!

I felt as though I was having a heart attack. My heart was broken. I went back to the house to confront him and he said he thought he was chatting with a woman. Then he said he never intended to meet up with the guy. Then said it was my fault because I had told him about the site. Then said this was not who he was and he was a better man than this and why don't I believe him and why don't I forgive him.

That night I made him give up all his passwords for the family computer. I logged onto his email and found all sorts of nonsense that had been going on for years. I found emails, websites, chat rooms, and photos from women and men. Apparently when I had moved out is when all of this started. In hindsight, I believe it was long before then. We divorced eight months later.

A year ago he met a woman eight years younger than him. They are engaged to be married, and she has now moved in. I believe she knows he is bisexual and is okay with it. He's no longer my problem. I did not tell anyone about this for six months. No one would have believed me, anyway.

Nancy's Story

I was a divorced mother with 2 small daughters, when I met my second husband. I fell in love with him instantly and he fell in love with me. We were best friends and married for almost 20 years until the day he spoke five words that changed our lives forever. "I am questioning my sexuality." I was in shock. I planned on growing old with this man and enjoying our grandchildren that we have. The first 15 years were great, but when my husband turned 40, something inside him changed.

At first I thought it was just a mid-life crisis, and that he would work through it. There were really no red flags at that time that stood out except that our sex life diminished. He blamed it on blood pressure medicine, drinking too much, and stress. All of those things were happening, so I saw no reason to doubt him. He was so in love with me and was my best friend. This makes it ever so hard to split up.

One night my husband was waiting for me after work. He said we needed to talk. He told me he wanted to move into a nearby hotel for a few days because we seemed to be drifting apart. He worked second shift and I worked first shift, so that always took its toll on us. I said it was fine if that's what he needed. A few days later he came home, but I could tell things seemed wrong.

He said he came home because he wanted to, not because I told him to. I thought that was odd. He started walking every day and lost more than a hundred pounds in about six months. He was overweight, but once he started dropping the pounds he couldn't stop.

A short time later he was diagnosed with depression and given medicine. His drinking increased even when he was taking his anti-depressants. He just didn't seem happy. The more I showed him love, the more caged he felt. He just didn't seem to be the same person anymore. He was not funny or loving, and I had no clue what was up.

Finally one month later, he moved out and took an apartment close by for six months. Those six months were the hardest months I have ever lived through. He would come over to do his wash or wash his car; he seemed to be pulling farther away from me and our son. When I look back, maybe he didn't come over as much because he was finally trying to separate himself from being a heterosexual man into a gay man. The more he came over, the more he would miss his old life. I'm not sure, I'm only guessing at this.

We went from yelling at each other to crying. Nothing made any sense, until one day I opened one of his credit card bills and saw a charge which I didn't recognize. My daughter checked and told me it was a Gay Men's web site. My heart sank, I called my husband and at first he denied everything

He said someone must have used his card. But after he arrived at our house with a large whiskey in hand, he later confessed he thought he was gay.

Unless you go through this, no one can ever really understand the pain and sadness you feel. You feel like your whole life was a lie, you don't even know who you are anymore. You start reliving every place you went as a couple, and what was your husband really doing. You just don't know what was real and what was a lie. You start to second guess who you are. I never thought I could feel such sadness and emptiness.

I filed for divorce one month later; our lives have never been the same. I went from yelling at my husband on the phone to crying, up and down emotions changing as fast as the wind. I couldn't sleep or eat; nothing seemed to help.

My husband had his own credit cards, and by the end of our marriage, he had maxed most of them out. When he moved out, he paid nothing for the whole year that he was gone. I continued to pay the mortgage, the second mortgage our son's braces, his school tuition, and his tutoring. Everything fell on my shoulders.

In those first months after my husband moved out, he asked me many times to help him with bills, I did. Later I finally realized I just couldn't help him anymore. I didn't care if he had gas for his car or cigarette money or money for brandy or even his rent. I paid his rent twice in the year he was gone and his car. Finally I just didn't want to help him anymore. I really hoped he would bury himself in all his bills.

Last I heard he was about 2 months behind with all his credit cards and still does not contribute one cent to his son. It's funny that my husband claims he wants to be back in our son's life, but I'm the one preventing it from happening.

The real problem is it takes a lot of work to re-build a relationship with a child. When you leave, it's not an overnight fix. It may take years before my son wants to see his father, and if I am honest, it really doesn't bother me so much. I try and surround our son with family that cares about him. Some people will disagree and say Nancy, you have to force your son to see his father, but do you know how hard it is to force teenagers to do things? He's not 4 or 5 where you can say your father is coming so get ready. My husband did come over on two different occasions, but when my son heard his father's voice, he ran out of the house down the street. He told me on several occasions when I asked him if he would call his father or see him because his father really missed him that, "Good--let him see what It's really like to miss someone.

Our 13-year-old chose not to see he father anymore. I did tell him why his father left but he assured me that the reason he didn't want to see him wasn't because his father is gay. Our son just couldn't understand how a father could leave their children. So it's been about four months since our son has seen his father; he won't even take his emails or calls.

I did take him to some therapy sessions, but we never made any headway. Our son is very stubborn and has chosen for now to cut his father out of his life. He said maybe someday he will want to see him, but for now no. A little part of me is happy with that. I won't lie. The thought of our son spending time with his gay father makes me nervous. At a time when our son is trying to figure out who he is I didn't want his father's sexuality to be an issue.

I also went to a great deal of trouble to hide what had happened in our home from our friends, I knew that most of them would be shocked, and I was concerned about any teasing at school. I only confided in a few friends, and some of those really dropped their friendship with me because they just didn't know what to say. I didn't blame them really even I didn't know what to say.

I know that you can't catch being Gay, and if my son came home someday and told me he was, I would still love him, but that is not what his father did. His father knew who he was 20 years ago and chose to marry and have a child 20 years later it's not fair to destroy your family because all of a sudden you want to live as a gay man. Our divorce should be final this summer.

Ten months after I filed, the only thing that has saved me is I was the breadwinner. Now my husband thinks he should be awarded some kind of alimony so he can continue to live the lifestyle he had with me. That one I will fight until I die I will never give him one penny to live his new gay life. Our communication is over; each time we try and talk it turns into a horrible fight with a lot of mean words tossed at each other. I don't know really if I will ever be able to talk with this person I called husband. My husband died--this new man is someone I don't know nor care to know.

You try and surround yourself with your family or friends and try and remember you did not cause your husband to turn gay. My husband told me that many times, if you had only been there for me and didn't spend so much time with the kids and grandkids then my inner demons would not have come out. This is a lot of crap!!! No one can cause another person to be gay. It's inside of them. My husband was never mature enough to communicate with me and still isn't. He continues to blame everyone for his choices. Finally in the end, we all have to decide how to get through this nightmare and what works for me.

Maybe it won't work for anyone else. I removed every picture of my husband in our home and tore up each wedding picture. There is no trace of my husband in our home. It helps a little. It helps not to see him anymore or talk anymore but the pain and sadness still remain. They say your pain just dulls it never really goes away.

I think about how nice it would be to date someone again, but at 57 it pretty scary. For now taking care of a teenager about to start high school is all I can handle. Some days are okay, but on some days you just feel like crying all day. Your life will never be the same. If only these men knew how much damage they were doing when they got married and lied to themselves and their wives most of which turned out to be their best friends.

Some people say just wait in time you will be good friends again. That is one thing I do hear a lot, and it's the one thing I have the most trouble with, because I don't want to be best friends again with this man. I only wanted my life back the way it was and it just can't be. That is the hardest part for me to accept.

It's been almost one year since my husband has seen his two grandchildren, not because my daughters wouldn't let him, but rather because he never really tries to see them. He always blamed my daughters for the amount of time they took from him.

In the end my husband lost everything, his wife, his son, his home, friends some family members all because he couldn't say who he was 20 years ago. And still to this day, he doesn't know who he is at 46 years old and still laying blame for everything that happened on everyone except himself. I wish I could say that there will be a happy ending someday, but I'm not sure I believe in happy endings anymore.

Sarah's Story

I have lived a bifurcated life, the distinct sides of which I now turn over in my hands as I write this. I am not young any more, and sit with my thoughts through sleepless nights waiting for closure and healing. Gene Robinson (first openly gay man to be appointed Episcopal bishop in the U.S.) said with certainty, "Love wins. Period. Love wins." I cling to that whole truth. I wake every day reciting the words, but may not be able to see it happen in my case. After nearly a half century of marriage, I have learned that John has always known he was gay. When I finally dragged open his closet door he said, "I married you so that I could be straight." Not much of a message of affirmation. When he said it I had the feeling that he felt I was the one who failed.

On one side of the bifurcation lay the magic: John was the center of every party, every peer or work group, and every committee. He organized every social engagement and infused fun into every event. Elaborate pranks and loud laughter, sometimes ribald, followed him always. Conversation never lagged when John was in the room. Early in our marriage we learned card games, and his quick intellect found that of all the games, bridge was his game to own. I became his partner in bridge marathons, his tagalong in social bridge.

He brought this same energy to our household. He kept the books down to a penny, using a huge black ledger. After a few years of traditional household roles, he began to do the laundry and grocery shopping. "It's a good match for my anal personality. You're too random to do it right," he declared. To me fell the cleaning, cooking, and the daily worry about the children's well-being. Together we gardened (did we ever!!), worked at church, and became pillars in the small community in which we lived.

It became a habit of mine to think of the half-full glass. I would look around at other marriages and say to myself that I had it better than most. Money was never a problem, due to our constant work and frugal habits, not to mention my hesitancy to demand anything for myself, so we didn't ever fight about money. We actually didn't fight about anything, until his epiphany changed everything in the happy little cocoon we had created. Mostly he planned our lives and I did the hard physical work to make it happen.

John was physically expressive to everyone outside the family. His hugs were notorious at church. We teasingly told him he was always "running for mayor," when downtown, as he easily made connections with people and remembered the names of everyone. His relationships at work were open, collaborative, and his work as a professor was rightfully praised.

Tolerance and indulgence of friends, no matter their beliefs and behavior, was absolute. A friend must never be offended by a challenging conversation about anything. In fact, hot topics were to be avoided totally in favor of talk about family, outsiders to the immediate circle, and about work. I was frequently reminded, on the way to a social gathering, about the political views of the guests, so that I would guard my liberal tongue. About outsiders and my family of origin, he was caustic and judgmental.

John loved to organize events around food. Going out to eat was a hobby. He would do the work of calling a group of friends, name the restaurant and time, and off we would go. Or even better, he would call friends who played bridge, ask them for dinner at our house and then we'd play a full night of 48 hands before having a dessert. The down side of his food obsession became a yo-yo diet cycle that sent him up or down the scale by 70 pounds. He would lose 70 pounds on diet pills in a rush to be thin, and then gain it all back in a compulsive binge that involved sweets after every meal. On one diet he gave up sugar and we all lived with the resulting blinding headaches.

Family Christmas celebrations became elevated to sacred events. Each year the children would choose a new outfit.

Stockings were hung, trees decorated with ornaments that were saved in individual boxes and added to annually. A standard dinner menu evolved, and friends and family rounded up for the Christmas Eve eating and storytelling extravaganza. Each family member was expected to come up with a talent, and that talent shared between courses and gift giving.

We had nothing to fight about.... Or did we?

On the other side lay a very different life reality. As John's wife I began to feel that I was the main prop in his plays. Instead of challenging him early on, I did what I believed was expected of me: I held a mirror up for him so he could admire his organized, happy, and controlled life. Many years later, after the epiphany, I was able with the help of a friend to put a label on his behavior: narcissism. He busily controlled every aspect of his life, and therefore my life as well.

I always worked full time, and was secretly pleased (and guilty for feeling that way) when my career took me to a workplace where he wasn't. In those places I could be who I was, free of people saying, "When is John coming?" In fact, in those places John didn't exist, and I thrived. Yet I always managed to meet the needs he was determined I must tend. One particular vignette stays with me: I was traveling around the state giving workshops from Sunday through Thursday. Thursday's workshop was several hours away, and I was the driver of record for the trip, so that meant I would drop the car off after delivering the other colleagues to their door, pick up my own car, and then drive an hour home. The next day was "Fat Friday" at his workplace, which was important to John, and he'd asked the previous week if I would make a particular pie for him to bring. I knew I'd need to bake four of these pies when I got home that Thursday, and I'd agreed to do it, but I had no idea how late my arrival was going to be. I got home around 10 pm, and John was in a tizzy. He was furious, actually, that I would have "let him down" on this important occasion. Now I'd have to bake through the night! And I did! He went to bed, and I baked. Did I confront this craziness? No. I should have told him to head on down to the bakery for pies in the morning, but I didn't. That's my problem: I fed his craziness.

Sex was strictly controlled, and he wrote the rules: If it was after 10 pm and before 11 pm, if the kids were well asleep, if the door was shut, if the lights were out, the temperature right, and he declared himself to be well enough rested, then we might have sex. But the biggest rule of all, the one most perplexing, was the rule that we could not have sex *unless I was well rested... and he was the only one to determine if I was*!!! By our 40's sex was a very rare thing indeed, and by age 50 it had disappeared completely.

Much more painful than having no sex was having no personal relationship. I began to realize that he filled every single moment with activities that brought other people into our lives, no matter what the circumstance. An evening meal with just the two of us? Not okay... we need to invite a friend who is alone at home tonight! A vacation? Not okay to just go off with me. It became a family vacation, and best if several friends trailed along. *I internalized this lack of personal attention as a character flaw in myself, and anticipated a day when he would actually want to be with me!* How could this fun loving, gregarious man not want to be alone with me? I didn't think of him as gay. I thought of him as being extremely interesting and sexually repressed. It was *my fault* that I'd not found the right combination that would unlock his potential as a partner. My compassion grew as the years went on, and I became more and more like my own longsuffering mother. I worked harder and harder, perhaps to avoid looking at the half-empty glass.

I was caught in a web of making it right for John. When he was dieting, I was blamed if I made cookies. When he was binging, I was guilty if a good dessert was not available in the fridge. When he invited friends in for dinner, he praised himself for being such a good helper because he set the table, but had little empathy for what putting a meal together might take out of me, and even less sympathy for me if I appeared "tired" during a long night at the bridge table. A theme of his was, "Are you going to be rested enough to be alert at bridge?" I continuously beat myself up for being such a wimp, yet I'd just routinely spent 70 hours at a demanding week of work, commuted an hour each way, cleaned the house, cared for gardens, and carried a full load of parenting, church, and community obligations. The truth is that he could only see me as an accessory to meeting his needs. He had no ability to feel mine. I looked at a catalogue recently about "accessorizing," and realize that described John's use of me... I was an accessory!

The first time it occurred to me that John was gay came 25 years into the marriage when a high school friend of his came for a visit one Saturday afternoon. After lunch we sat on the back porch. The two of them began to exchange inside jokes and stories, and it occurred to me that neither of them was even aware that I was in the room. To test my theory, I left and did other things for the next hour. Upon my return neither of them had noticed my absence or acknowledged my return. I began to turn the novel idea over and over in my mind and concluded that yes, he was probably gay.... but that he was so repressed he couldn't possibly know it!! So our stately, even elegant life dance continued.

In our entire marriage we had never occupied a bathroom at the same time. He was obsessed about smells, particularly those coming from his bathroom, so bathroom spray was a most critical item on our shopping list. Foot powder to control any foot odor was equally important. His morning routine in the bathroom was rigid to the extreme: A visit to the bathroom, followed by breakfast, and then another time in the bathroom. Travel could only happen if he was assured that this schedule could be accommodated. The only travel we ever did together happened when the tour leader personally guaranteed that his immediate needs would be met. I experienced this behavior and chalked it up to the repression.

This was a man who hugged freely... everywhere but at home. On Christmas Eve, when he handed out generous checks to the children, he was prepared for a hug, and even expected it. But hugs just for hugging were never okay, especially from me. In my denial I even gave it a term: John was so repressed he lived in an acrylic bag, tightly zipped. I had compassion and experienced only private disappointment when he went off to counseling for depression and nothing changed.

This was the half-full glass I continued to hold until John finally came out to a single good friend. But the coming out was as strictly controlled as his entire previous life had been. He was completely in charge of his closet. He would open the door to a particular friend, to a support group, and to our pastor. But to me he simply raved about the religious epiphany he'd experienced, God's love pouring down upon him in a blinding revelation. John, the least risk-taking person I've ever known, started an affair with a good friend, a married man who attended the same church... and I was pushed ever further away in dramatic and even cruel ways. Ignorant of what was really happening, I begged for marriage counseling and was told that his best friend was the only counselor he'd ever need, but, "If you need counseling, go ahead on your own." Yet when I did seek counseling, he was incensed. He refused to take me to the airport for a business trip on the same day he offered to make a seven-hour drive to pick up a friend. He banished me from the bedroom by accusing me of having a snoring problem. He asked if I needed to go to treatment for alcoholism because I liked a glass of wine with dinner. He demanded that I endorse his generosity with his friends (which actually became an embarrassment. He took his friends on several cross country trips, gave extraordinary amounts to the church) while scorning my frugal lifestyle. He accused me of being self-centered because I refused to get involved with several daytime bridge clubs after I retired.

In the middle of all this, a grandchild appeared. Our daughter lived in a distant state. In the traditional manner of mothers, I planned to go down to help with the newborn and was surprised to hear John say, "Why don't you give them a year of help?" At the time I just felt relief! To actually get out of this house that was becoming a torture chamber was most welcome. After a few months as chief nanny I knew I would never go back, and John encouraged me to think of getting my own place. He had conveniently distanced himself so he could pursue his fantasies.

Yet I did go back occasionally, probably because I felt the need to continue the appearance. I'm puzzle about that. Christmas as a family? Of course! Thanksgiving, major birthdays, that kind of thing. It always went badly when I re-entered his world. He could no longer freely pursue his life – the affair, the gay porn, the men's Bible studies, the hours counseling with men – and also he had his expectations for pushing as many social events into those times I was home as he could possibly manage to schedule, leaving me physically and emotionally exhausted.

Last Christmas was particularly difficult. He was downright insensitive to me, and the tension between us was noticeable. After a service at church I was waiting for him to appear (he was praying with someone after the service) when his good friend sidled up to me. "Any chance I could have coffee with you on the sly someday soon?" was his question. "Hey," I replied, "That's the only way it would happen, because if John knew we were meeting he'd be right there with us. Tuesday is good for me."

Tuesday came. We sat, and I asked what it was he wanted to share with me. "I want you to know that I have come to you because I no longer can stand to see you go through what you're going through. You need to know that not only is John gay, but that he knows it and *is acting on it. In fact, he has a rather long term relationship going on.*" He told me that John had known he was gay since high school as well.

In that hour all my compassion left me, and a steely hard determination took its place. How could I have allowed this man to rob me of my life? By morning I had a plan to confront him.

The next day was typical. John was busy, busy, busy. When he finally came home late afternoon I said, "You and I haven't had a chance to talk, and I feel the need to do so. I want an hour of your time right now." Startled, he agreed, and we went into his lair, the TV room. I continued:

"I have two questions for you. First, I want to know if you still believe in no secrets. If I've heard you once, I've heard you a thousand times vow that we will have no secrets in this family. So do you still believe that?" He nodded his head and said, "Of course!" "Then, my second question is something I should have asked many, many years ago. Before you answer let me remind you that you just affirmed the no secrets pledge. I must ask you if you are gay." He didn't miss a beat, and said, "Of course I'm not gay!" To have this boldfaced lie right there in front of me ended our relationship. "I plan to divorce you because I know you are lying," was my response. He still didn't crack. And after another strained day, I returned to my second home.

Breaking into his phone records took about ten minutes on line, since we shared a phone plan. Ten minutes after that I had the name of the person with whom he was having the affair. Absorbing that startling detail took a bit longer.

And so I am divorcing him. A month after the holidays we were together again, and I presented the evidence. He didn't want to admit it, but he finally had no choice. In a sense I also forced him to tell the children, mostly by simply falling apart at a family dinner. He was a witness that night to my breaking heart, and he could avoid it no longer. In a further (and completely positive) loss of control, I confided in my closest and dearest friends. While he didn't want to do that either, he visited with each one of them and admitted what was going on. In that process, I realized John was only doing what he was forced to do in order to keep his life of high control together. More importantly, I finally realized that my voice is absolutely my own, not his.

Perhaps the biggest hurt I experience now, today, is that John is most upset not about my knowing and dealing with the knowledge that he is gay, but that his friend "betrayed" him by telling me, and that I am asking for a divorce that will result in his loss of control over all our finances. For him the "betrayal" weighs more heavily on him than my right to know the truth about his affair and about his deception. He has asked me repeatedly, "But we had a good life, didn't we? Isn't there another way we can get through this?" I know that is code for wanting to maintain control of our bank accounts and of the flow of information.

And that is where he wants to leave it, apparently. He does not intend to exit the closet beyond the toe he poked out. He says he won't allow anyone in our hometown to trash me when they hear of the divorce, but he also doesn't understand that is exactly what will happen when the word is out, and he will only look more saintly for defending me. He is in counseling, but I know from long experience that he is smart enough and enough of a narcissist to manipulate the counselor. Does it occur to him that the grace he has experienced with the children and the few friends (unconditional acceptance of his sexual identity even while clearly condemning his treatment of me) is just a taste of what his new life could be like if he completely exited the closet?

So will love win? What in my power can be done to allow love to win? I cannot any longer allow this man to control my life or my money, as I have allowed for so many years without any payback other than this pain. Will I be able to refocus on the good parts of our life once I have my freedom and gain control? Do I have it within me to walk away from this man and leave the rancor behind? In the short term I must be as tough as I have ever been, continuously restating what is right for me and how I must proceed. In the long term? Who knows? He never does anything to lead a parade, other than organize the fun. He is paranoid about being in a situation where people do not adore him and give him praise. The emotional blackmail that I can inflict on him is huge, but I know that he is betting (correctly) that I will not play that card. I know what is reasonable and good.... So I just have to continue to be tough in defense of myself and to state my position. Only then can love win.

What is forgiveness all about? Short term I must forgive myself for being such a doormat for this man. Long term I must forgive him for being just who he is: a narcissistic gay man in search of himself. Only then can we be together with the family.

The Stately Dance

Our dance was stately,
our purpose sure.
Loves greatest ambitions drove us,
or so I thought.
I measured my half full glass
using my sainted mama's rules:
Forbearance of fate, so sad,
long-faced. But kind!!
Do not speak of his small cruelties
After all, I have my own.
Be always charitable – agreeable!
The rules for sex were baffling, maddening,
Yet those we codified in the long dark
of furtive groping.
Practiced at cheek turning, I took up a mirror
and held it steady
He admired his own silver nitrate image
while he longed for another man
to hold it instead.
Arms tired, sometimes I cried alone on the commute,
while he found casual sex in the bushes
and wept with shame, alone.
My own longing for connection cut off
by work, by frantic balancing of reflections in one hand.

The other kept busy with cluttering time
to keep him busy! Happy!
My private labyrinth of reason told me he was gay.
But the acrylic bag he lived in said he knew it not,
nor could he ever. How could I challenge that?

Sunday's Story

It was autumn 2002 when I met my future husband, David, online at a wonderful global dating site that is now defunct. For that period of time in 2002, it was still rather unconventional to meet one's future spouse "online." It was the classic deluge of flower deliveries, romantic cards, and gifts that I experienced. I immediately went into a state of luminance because in my first marriage lasting 32 years, I had been regularly ignored, cheated on, and more specifically, verbally abused by a straight man with a highly addictive personality.

David seemed to be just my perfect Prince Charming. (Be wary of that adjective, "perfect"!) He was 49 and I was 54 when we met. I resided in California, and he was in the Midwest. He had been divorced for 10 years, had no children, and worked at a steady and stable job at the upper corporate level. We physically met about a year later and were married shortly after. I was overjoyed. I had finally met my soulmate.

I routinely began to ignore certain red flags; however, in retrospect, it was because I truly wanted this marriage to work out. As I look back, I remember feeling something was just "off" in the pit of my stomach after first seeing his photos for the very first time. He looked rather girlish or effeminate, even "pretty." I showed his photos around, and I voiced my concerns over it. But people told me he appeared to be very pleasant looking, even good looking, so I simply ignored that little nagging voice in the pit of my gut and proceeded to throw all caution to the winds. David called me 4-5 times daily just to tell me he missed hearing my voice or to say how much he loved me, and that I had made him so happy. He stated that I had "completed" him. We were indeed going to have a wonderful, happy, and fulfilling life together just as soon as he tied up all loose ends concerning his aged/ill parents and received his second university Master's Degree. He already had his MBA.

He wrote me the most marvelous e-mails, and sometimes, when I shared them out loud to those closest to me, I was told, "He's just agreeing with everything you say. He's just telling you what you WANT to hear." My first husband whom I met in high school had constantly been very argumentative and there was always much drama, strife, and sadness going on in our lives, including the death of our 18 year old son and our home subsequently being foreclosed on.

Being with David was like the proverbial "breath of fresh air," and I felt very safe and secure with him. However, when my adult daughter asked about whom David's friends were, I honestly told her that he had just one very close woman friend who was married, and she thought that was quite strange. It was my daughter's gaydar that kicked into high gear, and she explained to me that a lot of gay men would usually latch on to a (safe) married woman for a "confidante" out in the public eye. David seemed surrounded by all these safe women at his particular secretarial-oriented job and also in his Theology courses.

He rarely discussed his ex-wife, but when I pressed him about what led to the break-up of their 5 year marriage, he would only say that she was a "shopaholic" and only interested in the material things of life. Several other times he referred to his ex-wife as someone whose "cage" he did not want to "rattle." That should have been a major red flag to me right there, but I ignored it until one day I teasingly told him that we could not be married until I had lunch with her so I could get the real scoop on him and on their marriage. He looked mortified! I told him he was free to have lunch with my ex-husband as well for the same reasons.

Sisters, with online dating/marriage being as common place and prevalent now, I cannot stress how important it truly is to at least try to speak to the ex. This is because online dating gives one a very limited perspective and is mostly fantasy-based, and had I done this bit of important fact checking in a reality-based environment, I never ever would have married this "Thief of My

Time." Even if you do not carry it out, I would advise acting as if you intend to and just very carefully observe his reaction for there are far too many predatory gay men online looking for a straight woman to marry and exploit for a myriad of selfish reasons (as in my case, as a "Cover Wife"). Please don't be taken in as I was.

Another important thing I did after our marriage was to install a good key logger on our shared computer because the admitted "Open Book" of a man had suddenly become very secretive and protected all of his computer files with passwords when he finally came to stay with me permanently several years later. However, I did not know that David was also a computer programmer who had secretly re-configured our computer, so I was only able to record a certain amount of what he was up to. I caught him in numerous lies constantly. I began to suspect that he was gay when I saw several thumbnail photos of men and Gay Porn on his desktop.

Another major complication was his bipolar mental illness that finally came charging out in full blown manic episodes that still leaves me feeling so traumatized to this day. Of course, he would never admit that he was gay, but I really had to KNOW, so I simplified this issue by giving him a book to read about how we are born predisposed to our sexuality in a certain way. I created a safe environment for him to discuss his sexuality, but sadly, the furthest he would ever go, was to admit he was only "a bisexual."

I thought I was marrying a fully straight man. I also thought that I would just die when the realization finally hit me full force as to why he had lost all interest in me as an attractive and intelligent woman who was used to having an adequate/fulfilling sex life as well as expecting to be fully involved with a husband/partner who had talked in terms of "us" and of "our" future--as he used to do.

He spoke grandly about "The Golden Years" to come and filled me with much anticipation and with the expectation of finally having a happy and fulfilled life with a good and decent man. Who was this man who now gave his back to me in bed for almost nine months, chastely kissed me as if I were a sibling or a friend, and treated me as a roommate? I wavered between denial and anger.

I think it was the SHOCK and all the stages of grief that one goes through when she realizes that the man she have married is certainly not who he has represented himself to be--and can never be. For me, it was like slowly going up on the most wondrous elevator ride hundreds of stories high and then being suddenly being plunged into the blackest moments of suicidal despair when that realization hit me.

I had time to reflect for that one year after I kicked him out with the help of a really wise woman therapist. I began to remember and I re-hashed out all the red flag moments with her like how he had told me several years earlier about having a severe crush on another boy in middle school aptly named John. David wanted to have an "exclusive friendship with John." He told me how handsome and talented he was and how popular he was in school with both sexes (John had a steady girlfriend). When I really examined what David had told me about John, I realized that this was a teenage boy he was crazy-in-love with! I asked him what had happened to John, and it sounded like David was almost stalking this guy because John and his parents abruptly left the area, and he never saw John again.

Then some years later, David told me there was a two-week "vacation" to see the Grand Canyon with yet another nameless man "friend" on a train. This puzzled me because they were both in their late 20's by now. I queried my therapist, "Isn't this the sort of vacation one takes with a girlfriend or lover?" She agreed with me because it's not as if they were both going on a schoolboy outing.

Everything he had told me pointed to David actually wanting to be in the company of another man/men (like 3 cruises to the Bahamas, an extended fishing trip to Florida where he caught a huge sailfish, etc.) And we had yet to even go on our honeymoon though David had promised he would take me on a sleeper car train ride through the Canadian Rockies. I can't imagine such a scenario today of being trapped in a sleeper car with a wholly disinterested gay man going through "all the motions" of a straight husband--maybe!

He agreeably said the things that I wanted to hear, but there was no real action or any follow through. Later, it safely came out in e-mails that we continued to write each other, that he had actually shacked up with a man for two years, which was the man he had gone to the Grand Canyon with a few years earlier! I asked him why he did this because no straight man I've ever known would do something like this in order to "save on rent," not when he had just been given a huge promotion to management. Nor did it seem logical to supposedly sleep on the living room sofa for two years because it was a decrepit trailer in a very private location only accessible by a very rickety foot bridge.

It was always like pulling teeth trying to find out WHO he really was--or even WHAT he was. It's as if he handed me an enormous salad bowl full of tiny puzzle pieces and it was incumbent upon me to put them all together so I could finally say, "Oh, you are gay." Several of those puzzle pieces included David thoroughly enjoying wearing the lipstick I applied on him because he always wanted to have this "experience" and having his toe nails painted bright red as he squished his large pale feet into my medium size sparkly teal flip flops so I could take a photo as he wore my silky black robe, silver anklet, and 3 toe rings ~ the Works!

Its taken me quite a few years to come to the realization and acceptance that I indeed married a fraud of a gay man who has wounded me to my inner core, and it is my sincerest hope that these gay men who do willingly marry straight women will someday be prosecuted and held fully accountable for their deceitful behavior and actions.

David destroyed not only my life, but the life of his first wife with whom he promised to have a large Catholic family in front of their parish priest. As a means to furthering my healing, I also have joined a host of online groups that assist women with infidelity as well as going "undercover" as a gay/bisexual married man in order to learn how they teach each other various ways to deceive their wives.

I have since learned that a lot of these men who wear too-tight blue jeans and have that stench of toilets are "cake eaters" who lead dishonest and deceptive double lives not caring a bit how many women's lives they have ruined. Perhaps it lends more excitement to their lives to engage in sociopathic "duping delight" or they have other odd ulterior motives for not wanting to reveal their true sexual proclivities, but regardless, women today really need to be totally pro-active in finding out just WHO they have truly married.

Read books on this subject concerning gay husbands, join online support groups, and please don't indulge in magical or wishful thinking like "praying the gay away" stuff. The marital situation will only worsen over time and especially be wholly detrimental to our female psyche and general health-- especially as we get older. Examine your collective finances, install a genuine key logger that you must pay for, speak to the ex-wife/ex-wives, and do a thorough background search on his "friends."

Get screened for STD's. Do not allow him to "explain away" anything that causes you ANY suspicion. Go very quietly undercover. Gather up all of the facts and be cognizant of any (mounting) red flags. Knowledge is Power, Sisters! Take good care of yourselves because with all the deadly STDs, you cannot expect him to. He's not interested in YOU, remember?

I thank God every day that we never were young enough to have any children because I loved this man to the very depths of my soul. I wanted to have his baby (if I could have) and die in his arms one day. Not anymore! I wish all of you the very best.

Sienna's Story

I met the man who was to be my husband when we were in junior high. We grew up in the same tiny country town and were raised with the same strict Southern Baptist upbringing. Religion was the central focus of our lives. My grandfather was a pastor, my mother was the pianist at the local church, and both of our fathers were deacons. Despite the religious environment of my home, at school I was surrounded by guys who seemed to only want sex. These were the type of guys who would even joke about resorting to the use of date rape drugs and alcohol to take advantage of a girl. These were the stories I heard all through high school and especially college. This was terrifying for me, and I longed for the "good guy" who wanted to be my best friend, to get to know me and to love me and not just take advantage of me sexually.

Charlie and I met when we were young teenagers, and I had a crush on him from the day we met. He was not like other guys; there was something very different about him. I had dated some major jerks, and I had been through a lot of hurt in my high school dating years, but Charlie was my friend through it all. We both had siblings in the military, and we would cry together, worrying about them so much. Charlie understood me, and he was so comforting through all the hard times. He was so gentle and kind, truly my closest friend.

The summer after his freshman year of college, we had both just gone through really bad relationships. We were talking one day about just giving up on finding real love, when he began joking about how we should just marry each other because we were so close. Even though I assumed he was just joking, I remember my heart was pounding the whole time we were talking. I had loved him for so long and had always wondered if he might have feelings for me too.

That summer, we started hanging out more with our church's college group. The college leader began doing a bible study that summer about relationships, dating, and marriage. Our leader asked us to make a list of the qualities we wanted in a spouse. During the next class meeting, as we shared our lists, he and I realized we were describing each other perfectly.

It was fate. We began spending more and more time together, and our first official date was the Fourth of July barbeque at our church. It was then that we made it known to everyone that we were "together." We dated for two more years, and because we were raised in such strict religious homes, we did nothing more than hold hands and shared a few quick kisses (and we had to be sneaky about it). We were both virgins when we married exactly two years to the day of making our courtship official—the Fourth of July. Our wedding night should have been my first clue that something was wrong.

Being a virgin, I was terrified on my wedding night. But I did love him dearly, and I was excited that we could finally be together. Since he was a virgin also, I thought he'd be eager to have sex that first time. I assumed he'd be all over me. I could not have been more wrong. He made no attempt to have sex on the wedding night and very little after that. I thought maybe he was nervous, but he said that he knew I was scared and didn't want to pressure me. I thought, "Finally I have found a man who cares about something more than just sex and wants me to be happy! What a prince!" But still, way in the back of my mind, something didn't feel right. I could not put my finger on it. Being a virgin, I had nothing to compare this to.

For the next several months, we lived the life of typical newlyweds. We struggled to pay bills. We fought about money, family issues, and all the normal marriage stuff. But we also fought about very strange things. He argued with me about the way I wanted to decorate the house, what clothes I wore, and how I did my hair and makeup. He even did my hair and makeup for me sometimes. I thought this was extremely strange. Men were not supposed to know or care about such things, much less be able to do those things better than a woman! It made me feel stupid. But I thought it was just me, and that he would never intend to make me feel that way.

Not long after we married, he lost his job. That's when things became extremely stressful. Still, I considered him my best friend. He always made a way for us, and we always worked things out together. We would lie in bed each night and talk about our day, sharing all our fears and frustrations with each other. I was so thankful to have him to lean on. Then, we'd snuggle and I'd fall asleep on his chest. I loved falling asleep in his arms. Still, there was very little sexual contact. When we did have sex, it was always bad. He was never "there" during sex. He was always emotionally detached. Of course, I blamed myself. How bad of a lover was I? I wondered what I was doing wrong or why he just wasn't attracted to me. I felt so lonely.

Then in January, after we'd only been married about six months, I became very sick and was in bed for the next few months. By this point, our sex life was completely dead. I was sick and in pain, and as always he was very gentle and took very good care of me. But still, he was distant. Too distant. He took care of me, but in much the same way that a nurse cares for a patient's needs, with compassion yet detached.

He began to feel like a stranger and I felt so alone and confused. Then one morning I was lying in bed and he was in the shower when his iPhone alarm went off. I reached over to the nightstand to grab the phone and shut off the alarm. When I did, the last website he had been on came up. It was a story. I began reading and realized it was a sex story....a gay sex story. The main characters were clearly two men having sex. There was no other explanation. I couldn't breathe. When he got out of the shower, I confronted him and I honestly don't remember what was said but he gave some excuse and brushed it off. It wasn't what I thought....it was not big deal....I was overreacting. Was I?

Soon after this, I confided in a close friend who was a marriage counselor and told him I thought there was something horribly wrong in our marriage. I didn't go into detail, I was too ashamed. He referred us to a counselor friend of his. Although we were supposed to be going to marriage counseling, Charlie said he had some things he wanted to deal with privately so he went to the first two sessions alone. He would come home saying how good it felt to have someone to talk to, and I would think, why can't you talk to me?

During this difficult time, I was secretly confiding in a close friend, the college leader from our church who had done the relationship bible study with us. She was a dear friend and was like a sister to me. It had come out months earlier that she was a lesbian. Of course she had to leave the church. At the time, I was devastated and could not believe how she had lied and pretended to be someone she was not. I couldn't look at her the same way anymore, not because she was a lesbian, but because I trusted her and she had lied to me. But she was understanding and kind. She explained to me why she couldn't come out in our small town Baptist church. She just couldn't handle the rejection she would receive, from everyone including her mother. Her life would be ruined. As we talked, I began to see that she was still the same person I had always looked up to and had always loved. Being a lesbian did not change what a wonderful friend she was to me.

One day while she and I talked about all my marriage troubles, she said, "Honey, I'm going to say this because I love you and I want the best for you. I think Charlie is gay." I was devastated and I felt like the breath had been knocked out of me. But something in my heart knew she had it right. She just knew. She had known him too long and she was a lesbian, so she had been through a lot of the same stages of denial that she saw him struggling through. I needed to hear it from him. But I didn't dare bring it up.

Charlie continued to go to counseling sessions alone. He didn't want me there at all. One day he came in from a session and walked into the kitchen where I was. I was standing at the sink (I remember as if it were yesterday), and I didn't even look up as he walked up beside me. I said, "So are you going to say it, or do I have to?" I knew he knew exactly what I meant. He said nothing. I asked, "Are you gay?" His eyes welled up and with barely a whisper he mumbled "Yes." The very first thing I felt was a huge flood of relief. I thought "Oh thank you God, it's not me!" But in the next moment, reality hit me. We'd only been married for nine months, and my marriage was over. With this admission, my husband was gone forever. My best friend had deceived me all this time. I sobbed. I screamed. I felt like I was going to faint. Actually, I almost did but he caught me in his arms. Those big, strong arms that had held me up through everything, now he was the one who was causing the hurt. When I could breathe again, my very first question was, "Why?"

He said all the same things that my dear friend had told me, that because of how we grew up, there was no way he could come out and still be accepted. He risked losing everything. And he did want a family and children. Apparently he thought I was the perfect person to try to live this "straight life" with. But once he married me, he quickly realized he could not keep up the charade. I was starting to notice things, and I was blaming myself. He didn't want me to do that. He said he genuinely loved me, he just wasn't "in love," and that he had never had the feelings for me that I'd had for him.

I was crushed. But strangely enough, I began to understand and feel sympathy for him. I knew he risked losing everything when he came out. And he had to come out. Divorce was looked down upon in our families, and I was not about to take the fall for this. He would have to tell the truth. His coming out got the reaction we thought it would, with the exception that he was not disowned by his family. We expected that. They are not happy, but he is still welcomed around his family.

As for me, it feels like a nightmare some days, a horrible nightmare. Everything I loved and believed in was false, and is now gone. I am learning to accept that this is my new reality and I have to start over from here. Charlie and I are still friends, but ours is a strange relationship. It is hard knowing that he is in a relationship with a man. There are still things about gay relationships that I don't understand and some that are too overwhelming to think about.

I am trying to move on. I am a teacher, and my students give me strength, courage, and laughter each day. I adore them and I love my job. Charlie and I never had any children of our own and we were only married for a year before he filed for divorce. Actually, he filed two days before our first anniversary. That was the day I wanted to die. Some days, the fact that I don't have children makes me very sad, but then I think of those women who are raising their children in the aftermath of finding out their children's father is gay. I cannot imagine. My hat's off to each of you! You are stronger than I could ever be! I recently met a woman that was married to a gay man and has a little girl. I'm glad to have someone who understands, but I do not know how she manages it all.

I have amazing people in my life, including a few gay friends who have been very understanding and patient with me when I ask a million questions. I hope to someday find love again, and experience all that marriage and intimacy are meant to be between two people who are genuinely attracted to each other. Right now, though, that seems to be too much to hope for and too hard to think about. For now, I am just taking each day as it comes and focusing on me and my needs. I am surviving this day by day, and I'm so proud of myself for that!

Tracey's Story

In January 2009 my husband starting getting very ill. First it was cold sweats; then it was the thrush in the mouth; next he lost an extreme amount of weight. I did a lot of research of his symptoms and the word "HIV" kept popping up. We went to several doctors to find out what the problem was. One phoned our house, but my husband wasn't home. He said that my husband needed to go to the emergency room as soon as possible because his blood work came back with some concerning things. I asked him if he had tested for HIV he said no. I then asked him if he should have. Even then I had no confirmation that he actually had HIV, but all the puzzle pieces were starting to come together.

We went to the hospital where they said he had an enlarged spleen. They did a series of tests and sent us home. While we were sitting in the room waiting, I asked him if it could be AIDS, and his reply was, "Yes." But then not another word was spoken about this. The next day we received a call that he needed to go see a kidney specialist as his kidneys were almost at the failure stage. A few days later we received an appointment with the specialist. When we went for the appointment, he did several tests and met with Ken alone. A week later we went to his office to receive the results. In all this time, my husband never said a word! Not a clue; not a whisper!

On the day we went for the results, we sat in the specialist's office. My husband still said nothing! The doctor came in, asked him if he would rather hear the results without me. Hubby said no. The doctor tried to sugar coat it, but AIDS is AIDS. There is no way to make it sound good!

We drove to the lake where years of lies were divulged which included many bath house visits and two long term relationships. One was still going on! My hubby never told either relationship that he had a wife and children. The part that hurt the most was that he denied his children. How does someone not tell people about their children? The children were already teenagers. It is three years later, and they still don't know the truth.

I always said to him that I would NOT be the door to his closet, yet 3 years later that is exactly what I am. I have told a very few people. They are the friends that the hubby has no part of. Our friends that we socialize with together have no idea. His business partner who is a very close friend has no idea. His wife is one of my closest friends but doesn't know. I feel our relationship changing; she must sense that I am hiding something.

If I had to describe my husband's characteristics, it would include selfishness. I would also add narcissistic. He thinks that buying gifts is showing love, but then he complains that we aren't grateful. He is clear that he feels he is deserving of "good" thing. He has told me that if I was a better wife, he wouldn't have had to seek affection and companionship from others.

He had a strong mother who did everything for him. She was from Eastern Europe. He had a loving caring father and much older brothers. Outside of the home, everyone thinks that his life is perfect. Our daughter thinks he is bi polar. He gives the family the silent treatment when he is angry. Maybe he doesn't realize that the tone of his voice is very degrading almost to the point of emotional abuse. He never deals with issues; rather, he just gets mad, degrades, ignores, and then when he is ready, he pretends that nothing happened.

I too have pretended! I don't like confrontation and will do everything I can to avoid an argument. After 29 years though, I am starting to trip over the mound of avoidances under the carpet. It is too big to ignore now!!

We have two children; our son is 20, and our daughter is19. Our daughter is leaving us to move to a new province in order to go to the university. Alexandra has funnily enough always said that her dad attracts gay men. She has over the years asked me a few times if I thought he could be gay. It is easy to laugh it off.

Our son is done his schooling and currently still lives with us. But he, too, will be moving out this fall to pursue his career of fitness.

Why haven't I told them? I believe that is their father's "secret" to tell. But he is not telling them. I believe our daughter and he would have a much better relationship if he would be honest with her. She knows that he is troubled, and she is very much aware. Their relationship is a rocky one.....they are very much alike. They often go long stretches of times where they don't talk. Our son is more easy going and not as aware of tension. I worry that he might not be accepting of the news at first. I also think he will be very protective of me and be aware of the hurt his father caused me.

As for me, where do I even begin? I come from a broken home with very little communication and even less affection. I don't doubt my parents loved me and my sister though. I hold in my hurt and will do everything I can to avoid confrontation and arguing. I will get physically ill if I do get into an argument or even if I hear one.

The one thing that I always wanted was children. We tried for 10 years doing everything that was suggested including hundreds of doctor visits. After fertility clinics and many, many failed attempts, I came to terms with not being able to have children. We tried adoption. We had a boy that we thought was ours, but a doctor with more money adopted him out from under us. We were on several waiting lists, and I had finally accepted our fate. I became very ill and was rushed to the hospital.......I was pregnant! I was already almost 3 months along.

It was during my pregnancy when my husband started to come to terms with his buried feelings and began experimenting. I was so over the moon excited and caught up in my own joy that I didn't notice. After the birth of our son, I just got busy doing mommy things. At his six-month check up, I learned that I was going to have a second miracle in my life--I was pregnant again! This was my husband's ticket to more freedom in order to further experiment and live his second life. I was busy taking care of the kids that I had so desperately wanted.

When we found out his diagnosis I was afraid because he had NO idea when he might have contracted HIV, so our daughter COULD have had it. I thank God every day that both my kids and I are clear of the disease! This was the beginning of the end of the "happy" marriage and family that was the only thing I had ever wanted. I became absorbed in being a mom and raising good kids. My husband became more distant, living a double life.

Before I knew it, the kids were teenagers, and my husband was sneaking out at all hours of the night. He told me he had met a group of fellow photographers and was now going out with them to do "photo shoots." I believed him......or I didn't want to know the truth. The saying "hindsight is 20/20" is appropriate for how I feel now.

Below are some thoughts I journaled in the early days of my marriage to give you an idea of how I was feeling:

I feel:
- Crushed - like I am bleeding from every opening, and my body is making new openings to accommodate the torrent
- Like my heart is beyond repair
- Inconsolable
- The world is crumbling on top of me
- I am drowning and no one can save me

I lost:
- Happily ever after

I want:
- To tell the truth
- To scream and yell
- To feel unconditional love

- To feel special
- To be ME.......but who am I??

Why:
- Can't he see my pain
- Can't he be honest.....with himself, with me, with the kids?
- Can't I be honest with him?
- Am I afraid to hurt him after all the hurt he caused me?

How:
- Does someone who loves you, hurt you soooo much?
- Can someone be so selfish that they don't see your pain?
- Is he so blind to his cruelty?

I wish:
- I was stronger
- I could yell and scream
- I was afraid to speak the truth
- I could be happy
- I didn't live a lie

I know:
- He hurts too but is it because he wants a lifestyle I can't give him?
- He can't be responsible for being gay........but he should have been honest.
- He doesn't know what he wants
- He needs to be honest with himself

NOW

So here I am 3 years later, still living a lie, not telling my family, our friends, our children. He wants to continue living like this. Every once in awhile he spends an evening or weekend with his other life, but generally stays close to home pretending to me, himself, and our kids that we are a normal family.

In year one and two, we went to many support/counseling sessions. I often was not completely honest as I didn't want to hurt him....why when hurt me so very, very much? In this last year we haven't done any sessions. We actually don't communicate much. We just live our lives and pretend that all is good. When we were doing the counseling, our relationship was actually better than it ever had been (aside from me now being the one who wasn't being 100% truthful).

What lies ahead is the question that is always on my mind. Our kids are both moving out and on to the wonderful lives that I know they have ahead of them.

Questions I need to answer:
- Is this enough
- Do you want a marriage without sex (I have no desire to ever chance being exposed to his disease)
- Do you really love him
- Is this enough
- Do you want to continue lying to your kids (after always teaching them that lying is wrong)
- Do you want to continue waiting for him to be honest
- Is this enough
- Can I afford being on my own
- I have one life to live, is this what you want
- Is this enough
- Is the grass greener on the other side

I am afraid of change and being lonely. After 28 years, our routine is familiar. Deep down and when I allow myself to be honest with myself, I know that I need to move on and out. I often wonder if he is waiting for me to say, "Let's separate." This way he can say to himself and others that it was me who wanted out, and he tried.

My friends who do know tell me I am young and still have lots to offer and want to know how I can possibly stay. I still love him and at times feel sad that he can't come out of the closet and be honest. What a burden to bear knowing you aren't being honest to yourself or so many others.

I get stronger each day and I believe that once the kids are gone, that it will be easier to move on. That is my hope.

Wendy's Story

To begin, I need to go back to my earlier days, growing up in the 1960's, in a small town in Hawaii, and later the suburbs of Washington, DC. I was part of a traditional Protestant family, being the fourth of five children, with both older and younger siblings. Although there was not much visible affection between my parents, there was always mutual respect and no sign of strife. My parents were good providers with a typical no-nonsense, approach, who focused on instilling in their children good values, responsibility, self discipline, and the importance of education and "doing the right thing." We also enjoyed a good measure of fun family time, from picnics on the beach to camping in the woods. Without question, I aspired to be an educated wife and mother one day as my mom had been. I just didn't know marriage would be so tricky to obtain and maintain.

In looking back, I have concluded that in spite of my parents' best efforts, I became lost in the shuffle of older and younger siblings (all high achievers) and hard working parents who had little time to nurture us individually. As I approached the teenage years, I found myself to be a strong student (as was expected) but socially awkward and shy, feeling unattractive (I had long thick wavy hair, that I wished I could make smooth and silky) and lacking self confidence ("I can never be as accomplished as my older siblings"). I longed for male attention, as most teenage girls do, but the thought of it coming my way frightened me. This self concept stayed with me through my college years, where I had enough friends and social activities, but no dating experiences to speak of.   In the early 1980's, while in my early 20's I moved far from home, moving in with former college roommates who had also migrated south to find teaching jobs. My new life had begun, and I thought I could escape my old, uneventful one. We tried out clubs in the big city, which never really were to my liking and both of those friends soon married, leaving me on my own once again. I eventually joined a church singles group, where I tried to hide my lack of social experience. I forged new friendships, but again, mostly with other young women. My longing for male attention still haunted me, but I lacked enough confidence to "put myself out there." For some reason, I still was intimidated by self confident men ("What if they found out how inadequate I was?"), so I carried on with group activities, wondering if I would ever find "the one," or more accurately, if "the one" would ever find and/or want me.

I joined the church choir, and enjoyed belonging to a group that had little social pressure. I grew to respect the choir director, who was also a full time music teacher, as he seemed to value high expectations and quality results, as I did in my own classroom and in my general outlook. I could tell he was a busy man as he rushed into evening rehearsals with fast food and got down to business immediately. I felt no attraction to him, really, but perceived his values and the dedication to work as similar to mine. After all, he was at church every Sunday! He was friendly enough, but we only talked occasionally, about work, as we taught in the same school district. Mostly, the older ladies would mildly "swoon" over him, being the 20-something unattached bachelor that he was.

Four months after I joined the choir, he called me out of the blue and asked me out. I was shocked, and remember immediately calling a girlfriend, saying, "You'll never guess...." I was too elated to question anything, and excitedly planned what to wear. After all, this was a man who looked so good on paper: established teacher, as I was, (a noble profession), same religious views, dedicated to hard work and quality results, respected by many, impeccable manners, mature, masculine, stable (He even owned his own home!), independent, intelligent, and a real gentleman (not a flirt). I learned that he was four years older than me, which was fine as I seemed to always be older than my years.

We immediately had easy conversations, and I was amazed to learn how closely our interests and values aligned. Although he was an only child, he appeared to have had "good parents" who had given him similar experiences, and he assured me that he was never allowed to be "spoiled." Needless to say, I was smitten almost immediately. The fact that he took things slowly attracted me even more. I felt he was genuinely interested in me as a person, not just as a woman, and I fell hard and fast.

Looking back, I think I fell in love with the whole idea of love ("Finally, someone really does want me!"), and never looked back. This euphoria resulted in my ignoring some things, although honestly it all looked so good "on paper" so it HAD to be right! To me, there was chemistry as well as compatibility. Though it all progressed somewhat slowly, I was relieved to not be pressured into anything I was not ready for and physical affection did move forward. I had nothing to doubt. At times he was not interested in hanging around after our dates, and I explained it away as his needing to be ready for his church job the next morning. Some of our dates involved going to school concerts, which he had to attend anyway, but I dreamed up in my mind that, "This is how it will be in real life someday, when we're married..." He worked long hours, often on weekends and late into the evenings, which I thought was the result of being ambitious, and having no one to come home to. ("That will change, when I am in his life.")

I now realize that I threw myself at him much more than he did to me, and again, the intoxication of finally being in love with a good man who liked me blinded me. I was so inexperienced, and yes, desperate, that I rationalized that "it would get better" when occasionally things felt a bit awkward. I learned that at one time he had been engaged but broke it off. He was reluctant to discuss it, so I did not push it. (I did not want the bubble I was in to burst!) I knew that she had been of a different religious background, so the break-up made sense to me. I now believe this confirmed for me, subconsciously, that he was indeed the "marrying kind," even though he was still a single man at age 30.

All in all, our relationship seemed so good, so right, and so normal. I was so desperate to finally have "my turn" at love and marriage, and my biological clock was ticking as well, at age 26. My family and friends were so happy for us! Within ten months of our first date, at the end of the Thanksgiving holiday spent at his parents' home, we were engaged although there was no actual proposal. Perhaps this should have been a huge red flag, but at the time it was only a minor disappointment. I suspected it was coming, but waited patiently. We drove back to our home town, went to the opera, then dinner, and then to my place. I kept waiting. I finally spoke up.

We had discussed marriage before, and I told him that if we did not want to wait until summer, we would have to get married over spring break when we both had time off, and that was only three months away. He agreed that he did not want to wait until summer, so that was that. We looked at the calendar, and March 2nd would be the day! No falling to one knee, no asking, no ring, no nothing, but I had my wedding date, and I was happier than I had ever been in my life, and oh, so naïve.

We continued to agree effortlessly as we purchased rings together, and wedding plans went into full swing immediately with only three months to prepare. Since we were both very practical, a bit older, and on our own, with parents out of town and out of state, we chose to put it all together ourselves. We decided to have the wedding in the church where he worked part time and where we were both established. As the bride, I was happy to take care of the arrangements pretty much on my own. He seemed willing to participate in the bridal registry process, etc. and I remember thinking how "right" this all was going to be, as we worked our way through to the actual wedding day.

I have since scoured my brain over the course of the past few years, looking for missed "gay clues" in the personality of this man and have come up short. He dressed nicely, but nothing over the top and was definitely not into fashion. (I was to learn later, that most of his wardrobe was chosen by his mother, not him.) He loved cars and knew everything about every make and model, and he could do minor work on them. He loved his hometown football team, and although this team was the arch rival of mine, it still meant he was a regular man who liked sports. I liked the fact that he was not super-macho or full of male bravado. For me, it was refreshing to see that he was not into pick-up trucks and hunting as many men are where I live. He was a musician, yes, but showed NO clue of flamboyancy or Liberace-type mannerisms which at the time was the stereotype for gay men.

I learned later in our marriage about a few of his colleagues who were gay, living a quiet, private lifestyle which was not really discussed. They showed no signs either other than being single. He made no comment, pro or con, about their orientation, and I liked the fact that he was as accepting as I was. At that point, I had little knowledge or personal experience with gay people myself, but I always believed it was not a choice, and not a matter of right or wrong. My Protestant church upbringing never involved any information or judgment about this lifestyle. I really knew nothing of the existence of homo-sexuality until I was in college in a Human Sexuality class. Studying child development, with lots of psychology thrown in, the whole "phenomenon" was a bit fascinating to me. Little did I know that it would one day be staring me in the face.

Other than the lack of a proper proposal, I felt that I had had my fairy tale ending, finally. I had married a strong, trustworthy, kind, and decent man, whom I loved, and we both looked forward to spending the rest of our lives together, as our parents had. For the first time in a long time, I felt "normal" and "acceptable." Though he was still learning, I felt loved, and just knew it would grow deeper over time, it had to. "How could it not?"

He planned the honeymoon as a surprise, keeping it secret until we arrived at the airport. At the time I saw it as a romantic gesture, but later concluded that this was more his way of keeping control. Ironically, we went to San Francisco! It was disappointingly cold, but we took it in stride and stayed busy seeing lots of sights. We stayed in a quaint older hotel, and in my mind I agreed with his being frugal and practical with this choice. I can't say there were fireworks physically, but given our lack of experience, I believed we had nowhere to go but forward. I had a man who had just chosen to marry me, and that was more than enough for me.

By the fourth night, he subtly and gently, but clearly indicated that he was not really interested in seeing me in another new nighty. I quickly figured out the rest and said nothing as I crawled into my side of the bed and sought sleep. That instant of rejection seared through me like an ice pick, leaving me with a mixture of surprise, disappointment, and confusion. I tried to make sense of it. "Is this normal?" "Well, we did have a very busy day...there's always tomorrow..."

For me, subconsciously, it had nothing to do with him, but rather it had everything to do with me. That moment affirmed all that I had always believed about myself: that I would always be subpar, something that was ingrained in my being. Still caught up in the whole idea of love, wedding, and honeymoon, ("This is really happening for shy, unattractive me!"), I tucked that scenario into the far back reaches of my mind, and quickly forgot about it--sort of. This was one of many seeds of shame to come which would eventually bloom into full blown depression for me twenty years down the road.

We returned home where we spent the rest of the week moving all of my belongings from my apartment into his home. Not only had I gotten a good man, but I now had a fully furnished home. Finally, at age 28, I was able to "play house" in real life! It didn't matter to me that the décor was eclectic—we had all the time in the world to refashion what was now OUR home! It was homey enough, complete with copper molds placed evenly across the space above the kitchen sink. At the time I did not see this as another indication of his mother's dominance in his life.

The next year went by uneventfully as I recall, with both of us working hard in our teaching careers. He had changed schools and was working on his master's degree in the summers while still working part-time with the church choir. He was now at a different church which was our social scene. I enjoyed being the choir director's wife at Wednesday night rehearsals and on Sunday mornings.

I believe this is where my co-dependency began. While I gladly took on the traditional role of wife, regularly packing home cooked lunches and dinners, I was also his "co-pilot," riding the coattails of his talents and sharing in the admiration and respect he received, in both his school and church work. He continued to work long hours, often into the late evening, and that did begin to bother me. I partly understood his dedication and commitment to his work, but a piece of me began to wonder where his priorities were. I had never been "number one" in anyone's life before, so I was unsure of what was "normal."

As a girl growing up in the '60's and '70's, with a mother raised a generation before that, I had learned early on not to make waves and not to make demands. My role was to take care of everyone else and put my needs on the back shelf. So another seed was sown, letting me know that I was not really number one, even in my marriage, and I expected nothing more, for the most part. The hurt that followed every subtle example of this, and although quietly tucked away, it never left me.

After many lonely evenings, I began to read books on young marriage, trying to glean tips on what to do to make it all work better. I prayed for help continuously. Though I did not see it clearly at the time, this was when his "victimhood" began to show its colors. It frustrated me that no matter how hard my days were teaching Kindergarteners all day, his days had always been worse. Being the supportive wife with low self esteem to begin with, I let him have his pity parties over and over again.

Following advice I'd read, I tried talking and communicating *my* needs. In most of these attempts at conversation, he was extremely defensive, and became a master at twisting and manipulating the issues at hand to the point that I felt wrong and guilty for bringing them up. There was always an important reason why he had to be at work, especially as I watched him climb the ladder of success and notoriety. After all, his success was now my success, too, and his ambition was one of the traits I admired in him. "Who am I to question a hard working successful man?" My codependency had found fertile ground, and I was on board with all the attention he brought to both of us, in spite of the hurts that came with it. Little did I know how my buried resentment would one day grow to consume me.

I was quite taken with his parents, who showered me with gifts at Christmas and on my birthdays; they were of a higher quality than I had ever received. His father was in the same profession--and very highly regarded in his field--so we met twice a year at conventions, along with making trips to their home for all of the holidays. Since my family lived much farther away, there were only brief yearly visits with them. Having only one son, I was the daughter his mother never had, and she loved discussing recipes and sewing projects with me. She exuded a level of class and sophistication that I had not experienced, and it felt good to be in the fold with folks who seemed to have more than I'd ever had.

Over the years, I came to realize how naïve I had been in those early days. Her lavish gestures were in reality her way of dressing me and controlling me, and I eventually came to realize how deeply she had affected my husband over the years. Both of his parents had strong opinions about how things should be, especially about their son's success. I learned that although he wanted to be a lawyer, they had chosen his profession and insisted that he live at home for college attending the school where his father was highly regarded. She was always very cordial to me, but I began to see signs of what his growing up years must have been like—very controlled, with unrealistic expectations--and little as far as nurturing. I perceived an insecurity about her, which she thickly covered over with a pattern of obsession over appearance and achievement.

To outsiders, she was revered as a classy and devoted wife with an accomplished husband and son. It became obvious why he had left his hometown and moved across the state for his first job. But they followed, coming to visit only when there was a concert or competition and keeping close tabs on the rising success of his performance groups. His ambition, in part, was subconsciously due to his inner child trying to avoid the wrath of his parents' criticism. Again being a nurturer, I decided I could help ease this inner pain that was never consciously acknowledged. I had married for better and for worse, in sickness and in health.

I will never know when my husband began to experience homosexual feelings. I can confidently say, though, that when he did, most likely in childhood, they were swiftly shut down and hidden deeply into the far reaches of his soul. I can only imagine the pressures he felt as his parents raised the bar continuously, and made it crystal clear how he was to be. Today I look at his childhood photographs, where he's all dressed up in coordinated outfits and posed just so, and my heart goes out to this little boy who was never allowed to really be himself. He had to comply with his mother's wishes in every aspect of his life in order to survive. It is no wonder he became a workaholic, needing constant outside recognition in order to feel okay on the inside.

Two years after our wedding day, our beautiful daughter was born! Another tiny seed of rejection was sown the day after I delivered and was recovering from a C-section. That morning he drove downtown to see us, only popped his head in to see me, and immediately went down the hall to see our baby in the nursery. I had barely seen her myself! It is interesting to me, the impact of that small action, in light of all the other little seeds that had started to sprout. I felt I had moved down another rung of the priority ladder though I never consciously thought it.

At first he involved himself in parenting more than I thought he might once he got the hang of it, and I was relieved. His long hours at school continued and when the baby was about six months old, I somehow mustered the courage to put my foot down about his part time church work which was consuming his weekends. I was saddled with all the parenting and housework on top of my own weekend teaching prep work, and it was just too much. Our income without this extra job was adequate. I sensed him using it as an excuse to pull away, but didn't understand why, especially having an adorable baby that he hadn't seen all week.

Now, I see this immersion into work, not yet an addiction, but a way to stay so busy that you don't have time to hear your tortured soul or see your wife ever so subtly slipping away. He agreed reluctantly, but over the years reminded me more than once how much he missed it. Again, victimhood.

Around that time we learned from his mother that his cousin, a medical doctor married with two young children, had left his wife because he was gay. This was so puzzling to me, but I noticed how remarkable it was that the family continued to include both he and the ex-wife in all family activities, and it was never discussed again. My husband also has a cousin on the other side of the family, a "confirmed bachelor," whose orientation was understood but also never discussed.

During this time my husband finished his master's degree, thanks to my typing his thesis, before the days of word processing and computers, with a little one underfoot. He moved back up to a high school position and we moved to another city. I was glad to now be in a home that we purchased together, and I thought a new life might breathe fresh air into our "okay" marriage.

Within a few months, I was pregnant with our wonderful son! I just couldn't believe I had been blessed with a girl and a boy, both healthy and just perfect. Occasionally in my mind I expected something to go wrong with my second child. My "subpar" mindset led me to believe I didn't deserve perfection twice. As most experienced parents know, one + one = more than two when it involves having children. I was juggling so much, still working full time, but we had a great babysitter and raising little children was another dream-come-true for me.

We now lived less than an hour from his parents, which concerned me at first, but it made for shorter visits and no overnight stays. I found the pattern repeat itself, where his mother lavished our children with gifts and especially nice clothes. I was most appreciative, but I realized as the years progressed that it was more about how they looked in public and what they achieved, than a true connection with the children themselves. It all became clearer to me how my husband had become the man he was, and I was determined to soothe his inner pain.

He soon began to get restless in his job being the third in line on his staff, after having been the head director in years past. I agreed that his talents were being wasted where he was, and within two years, he landed a head position, back in the suburbs of the city where we'd met. So, I was packing up the house again, now with two young children in tow and hoping I would find a job for myself when I got there. There was more hope that things would improve with another new start.

In writing this, I must say that he was always a good provider and did take on all of our finances as well as the traditional "husband chores." I really had nothing concrete to complain about. But now I see so clearly how the toxic patterns of our relationship evolved: Though I don't think he knew it on a conscious level, he was a master at rationalization, manipulating circumstances and conversations to remove all blame from him. I now believe this skill was developed in early childhood as a defense mechanism. I saw how he was constantly judging others and putting people down, in order to pull up his sagging inner ego, though, looking back, he was probably afraid to outwardly say anything about me.

In a sick way, I was partly a mother figure, the nurturing one he longed for, and he wouldn't dare risk losing that. However, in our marriage, it was always about HIM, which my codependency encouraged, and it eventually developed into narcissism.

At the time I excused it away as "being an only child." Yet in the bedroom he wanted nothing. No wonder I was confused and ashamed! There was also a clear lack of reciprocity, which I did not consciously see for many years. I gave and gave and gave, and he took and took and took, and rarely gave back, especially when it came to my emotional and physical needs. This eroded my soul.

I also saw similar negative patterns develop in his relationships with our children. When he did come home, they excitedly brought him their school papers or their latest creative projects. Often he rejected them, ever so subtly, telling them he would "look at it later." This broke my heart, but it also told me that the rejection was not just for me. We became roommates, and I felt valued only for the services I provided: housekeeping, laundry, child care, shopping, cooking, and parenting. I lamented over it all, in private, of course, but always concluded that it could be worse: at least he wasn't traveling out of town, we were financially stable (and he was handling all of that on top of his busy schedule), and he wasn't straying, except to work where he had become so respected.

It is also important to note that he *never* raised his voice at me or *ever* complained, or put me down. This came as a mixed blessing as I see it now. He gave me no hard evidence to be unhappy or want to leave him. After all, he was doing nothing obvious to hurt me. By all appearances he was loyal and devoted. It was a game he had learned to play long, long ago, to survive. I figured it would be far worse to be alone now that we had two children. At least on the outside we were a happy family, something I dreamed of my whole life. I convinced myself that I should consider myself lucky to have what I had.

Somewhere in the middle of all of this, I lost my mother to cancer. She had not responded to chemotherapy and lived less than a year after her diagnosis. Though she and my dad lived far away, we were in close communication through weekly letters and regular phone calls. Until she was gone, I did not realize how big of a role she had played in keeping me going. I never discussed my marital problems with her, but she did serve as a cheerleader of sorts, always interested in my work and my kids, in spite of having four other grown children with families. She filled a hole that my husband never did, and when her support was gone, I sank a little deeper.

Over, and over, and over again I believed there HAD to be a way to make this better, and it was my job to figure it out. I felt extremely responsible, yet incredibly inadequate. I read everything on marriage I could get my hands on and found myself riveted to every talk show that covered relationships. Shame rolled in, as I learned how abnormal our marriage was with him showing no interest in me physically, without explanation. How can this be? ("Oh yeah, I am unattractive, and have never been *enough*, my whole life. It's *me!*")

The talk shows and magazines *never* discussed husbands NOT being interested in their wives; I felt like a freak. Nor was the idea of gay men marrying straight women ever mentioned, and there was *nothing* to indicate that my husband was gay. I had never heard of such a preposterous phenomenon other than the fluke instance with his cousin. So there HAD to be something wrong with me—I was not overweight, so I couldn't even blame that! It had to be something terribly wrong with by being. Instead of my marriage bringing out the best in me, it confirmed all of my feelings of inadequacy. I felt so alone, and this was certainly too shameful to be discussed with anyone.

Instead of attempting talks with him, I began writing letters, to avoid him twisting my thoughts and feelings, as he did in conversation, and pointed out that this was no normal marriage, but I was willing to work together on it. I remember, out of desperation, writing the definition of "cherish" in one of my letters, trying to explain my need to feel this way and reminding him of the sacred vow he took to cherish me. More rejection followed, as often he didn't even acknowledge the letters. I was in a constant state of push and pull, trying to sort out whether or not he was capable of being in a loving relationship, and whether or not I deserved better. ("Should I stand back and be patient like an understanding wife, or should I express my concerns?")

I was brought up to not make waves, but tried to take advice I'd read and be brave and confront, in a civil way, of course. Occasionally when cornered, he would say, "I'll try..." but mostly he thought everything was *just fine* at home, and that I was demanding too much of him. This destroyed me more, but I pressed on, trying desperately to find a solution.

At one point, after ruling out an affair as the explanation for his lack of interest (he was too busy for that and was not the flirty type) I remember asking him point blank in a letter if he was gay. At the time I thought it impossible, but just couldn't figure it out, and was at my wit's end. Again, no response, but this may have stirred something deep in his tortured soul. I pressed on, as I had two beautiful children, who were, for the most part thriving, and who deserved better. I began to give up on God as my prayers did not seem to be heard or answered.

After close to twenty years of marriage, though withered, my spirit was not completely broken, and I finally began to think that HE was, at least in part, responsible for some of the demise of our marriage. I began to read about work addiction, which actually gave me great relief. THIS is what was wrong! Perhaps it was not all my fault after all. He fit the profile described, as his upbringing mirrored what I read about, and *finally* there was something tangible to deal with. To my surprise, he seemed willing to read one of the books I had read (and highlighted!).

In retrospect, it makes sense...anything to keep me going down the wrong path or barking up the right tree. He worked his way through it, without comment or discussion, except to use it as another factor in his cause and excuse for his own victimhood. Workaholism had swooped in on him, poor thing. His career was on fire, as his performing groups soared above the rest across the state, and he gained national attention, and even our daughter was now involved in his program. He would win one award and quickly make plans to go after another, pushing his students to excel and get him there, and in his mind he justified his demands as "doing it for the kids." He was addicted to approval and recognition, ever searching for the next fix. The hole in his inner child had a bottomless pit. He was sought after by many, doing consulting work on top of everything else, which soothed his sagging ego.

In spite of his success, he went through about 12 assistants over the course of about 15 years. It became embarrassing for me and my children as one after the other resigned at the end of the school year, unable cope with his demanding approach and expecting them to put in the hours he did. At home he became so frustratingly unreliable, canceling plans at the last minute to finally be home for dinner or breaking promises to do things with the kids as his need to control overtook him.

He was adept at bursting everyone's bubbles, in an attempt to shift the focus back to himself and was the epitome of "raining on others' parades." Yet he was revered and respected in the outside world. It was difficult to stand by his side in public, and listen to the accolades thrown his way, so I began showing up less and less or faked my admiration of him. The conflict tore at me, as I tried to deal with the importance of presenting a "solid front" with both parents, yet feeling for my children as they watched their father emotionally abandon them, and me.

I believe at this point that *perhaps* his repressed gay feelings were beginning to bubble up to a more conscious level, which I am sure tortured him, having been pushed down for so long and being so unacceptable in his mind. Together with full-fledged work addiction consuming him and having difficulty with colleagues, he began to topple under the stress, at least in the privacy of our home. He had more and more physical ailments, from chest pains, to headaches, to panic attacks, to dizziness, to sheer exhaustion, resulting in his returning to bed instead of going to work. He became the king of excuses and blame; however, NONE of this was HIS fault.

I urged him to get help, and he was given an anti-depressant. He attended only a few therapy sessions, stating he did not like the therapist. I had also discovered my full-fledged co-dependency through my readings and slowly learned to separate myself from some of this toxic entanglement, but now that he was "sick," I believed it was my duty to support him, as the vows I had taken so long ago still indicated. From the outside, one might wonder how I put up with all of this for over 20 years. I have wondered the same at times, but I have concluded that his 15 -18 hour work days were, in an odd way, my survival. Though alone, I definitely had my own space. It was the holidays that were so difficult, when he WAS home.

Meanwhile, my own work in the elementary classroom became more and more demanding and emotionally draining. Even as young as they were, the kids I was teaching now came with less interest in learning and more behavioral issues. Parents were more demanding to get their way, less respectful of me and how I was striving for their children, and from the top, there was increasing pressure for test scores. I found myself devoting more and more of myself to my students and less and less to my own children.

Weakened from my deteriorated home life and 20 straight years of teaching, I decided to take a year off, and my husband reluctantly agreed that we could afford it. Within six months, part time secretarial work from the school district fell into my lap, and though it paid far less, I found my life more in balance. I worked in an office affiliated with my husband's department and began getting to know many of his colleagues, many of whom were male. To my surprise, I found them giving me attention and warm appreciation, unlike I experienced at home, which saddened me but also showed me that perhaps I did deserve better.

Eventually I felt I had to return to the classroom, as the college years with financial responsibilities were approaching for my children. I found a teaching job in a different school with a new grade level, and there many changes, in terms of technology use, since the time I'd left the classroom four years earlier.

The whole experience overwhelmed me and as hard as I tried, I just could not cope with it all. Within ten weeks, I was crying every morning in the school parking lot, losing weight (not typical for me!), and barely making it through the day without falling apart. With no support at home, there was no stopping the major depression that had consumed me. I just wanted the pain to go away, and I saw no way out. The idea of ending my life kept swirling around me, though I knew I was too chicken to really pull it off. I had two beautiful children with a father who could not be there for them in my absence. I had visited suicide once before, after college, but escaped it by moving far away to a new life "down south."

This time, thanks to alert family members who saw my desperation, I went to a doctor where I was diagnosed with major depression and took a medical leave. I navigated through a whole new world of psychiatrists, therapy, and medication, and slowly got back on my feet. My husband had no choice but to go along with it, and most likely he let everyone know how hard it was for HIM to have this added burden. After all, my being home meant I had more time to take care of HIM.

That time period of a few years was spent trying to figure out my life and my issues and now seems mostly a blur. I do remember my first therapist inviting my husband in for a session, after I explained his work addiction, and she basically told him he needed to take me out to dinner more and all would be well. Needless to say, he was off the hook, and I changed therapists. She just didn't get it. I found my new therapist frustrated with me, as I tried to explain it all, but was too ashamed to discuss the bedroom. She didn't bring it up, nor did I, and I felt I was spinning my wheels, going over and over the frustrations in my marriage, but not really knowing what was wrong.

Medication did help me cope, and I can't say enough about how helpful it was as a ladder to get me out of the deep hole I was in. It did not make me groggy or a zombie though there were mild side effects, and it took awhile to get the right mix of ve of a teenager was supposed to do. Nothing but sports websites had ever turned up, but I kept viewing it from time to time. Then one night, there before me, one after another, were gay porn websites. Needless to say, my stomach turned and shock set in. I kept it to myself, checking again the next night when I knew for certain that my son had NOT touched the computer. I was in disbelief but was brave--and angry--enough to confront my husband. Of course he denied knowing anything about it, pushing the blame on our son. I was stunned. Feeling so alone in the world, having never heard of such a thing-- a gay man marrying and pretending to be straight—I went to the internet for research.

At first I found a website discussing the situation, and how couples just "worked it out" and stayed together. This seemed preposterous to me, a real cop out, which voided wedding vows. Luckily I soon found a wonderful source of support at

219

www.gayhusbands.com, and I began an enlightening and supportive email conversation with its founder, Bonnie Kaye. She too, had experienced this, and I learned that there are over 4 *million* women in this country alone, who find themselves in this situation. I came to understand that many men, who grow up realizing they are "different," repress these thoughts early on out of fear and shame. They want desperately to live a "normal" life and sincerely believe deep down that marriage will "cure" them. It works, for the most part, for a few years, or many years. This was my husband in a nutshell.

I printed the letter "Come Out to Your Wife," found on Bonnie's website and put it under his pillow before leaving for the weekend to pick up our daughter from college. I pushed harder, and finally after about a week of questions/denials, I got a letter from him, admitting some things. I was shocked, disgusted, disappointed, ashamed, and even a bit relieved to *finally* have a few answers, and some honesty. Then more questions fell from the sky, preoccupying my every thought. ("How did I not see this coming?") I held on to my communications with Bonnie for dear life, as I could not bring myself to talk about it for a long while.

What I did know immediately was that I would not live a lie and could not stay in our marriage. Our relationship had deteriorated on so many levels already, as his narcissism and work addiction had taken over. It surprised me that he agreed so quickly, and we discussed a plan to hold off until the end of the upcoming school year to separate and divorce. We had some of the most honest conversations we had ever had during those first weeks. But the shock and sense of betrayal and shame in not having seen this coming overwhelmed me.

I checked out books from the library and found a new therapist nearer to home since I knew I would need to see him regularly to cope with this new turn of events. I had to come to grips with all of this before dropping the "divorce bomb" on the kids, although it was obvious, at this point that our marriage had unraveled. Now having a handle on my depression, I knew somehow I could survive this as well.

That fall, I was advised to start dropping the seeds of our plan to divorce with the kids, so they could have time to adjust as well. I wanted to do this together, but my husband could not bring himself to do this even though we were NOT going to disclose anything else. So, once again, I had to take charge. I went to see my daughter at college, very briefly, just to plant seeds. When I returned, it was time to tell our son. Neither seemed terribly shocked, but I knew it would take time to absorb the news, so I decided leave it alone for awhile.

In the following weeks, I noticed him "missing in action" a bit more than usual. Returning home from visiting his parents or doing consulting work was taking longer than usual, and the excuses seemed lame. His defenses were crumbling. Though it seemed so farfetched for this highly professional man to be visiting adult video stores, I now knew anything could happen. My new advisor and friend, Bonnie Kaye, educated me on the frequency of such encounters. Though it disgusted me, I shrugged it off, thinking my marriage was already over anyway, and I thought surely he would not be bold enough to do anything stupid, as he had too much at stake.

In early November, a few weeks after realizing his new patterns, the next bomb dropped. One Monday evening, he called our son to say he was on his way home from work, a 20 minute drive. Two hours later I went to bed, wondering, but not terribly alarmed. The phone rang at 10:30 pm, and it was my husband, calling me from the county jail *in a neighboring rural county*. I was stunned once again. He explained that he was being kept there overnight (always the victim) and kept saying how sorry he was in between his requests for me to call in a substitute for him for the next day. He gave me the jail's phone number but implied that they or he would be calling me. I was in such shock, I didn't even ask about the charges before hanging up the phone.

Somehow I made it through the night and had to come up with what to tell my son, who had to face going to school the next day and the class where his dad was his teacher. I could not bring myself to tell him where he was, especially since I knew so little. I assured him that his dad was okay and safe. Somehow I made it to work and waited for the call.

By noon, I could not stand it anymore and called the jail. I was told that nothing would be happening until the judge arrived, typically in the late afternoon. I asked the clerk about the charges, thinking she would probably not be able to disclose this over the phone, but she nonchalantly stated, "Public Lewdness." I found myself in yet another tailspin.

After work he called, explaining that I would need to post bond and come get him that evening which I did. At this point I had to tell my son what I was doing and asked my sister to call and check on him after I left. During the long 45-minute drive, I carefully composed my words, thinking that now was the time for him to get some real help. He immediately went into defense mode, stating that "It is not what you think." I guess he had time to plot his words as well. All he would tell me was that he had gone to a roadside park to walk and had been mistakenly caught up in a sting operation, involving several people and how badly he had been treated. He briefly explained to our son that it was all a big mistake and got up and went to work the next day as if nothing had happened. In my heart of hearts I wanted to believe him, and I hoped this nightmare would be over as quickly as it had occurred.

By the end of the week, the principal appeared in my husband's office and explained that the school district had received two anonymous calls about what had transpired, and as a result, he was being put on administrative leave, pending an investigation. He was escorted out and that was that. My biggest concern was our son who found himself in the middle of this mess. Fortunately, having been a student leader that fall, he had gained both popularity and respect, and the kids and parents rallied around him, not quite knowing what was going on.

The school district came down hard on my husband, rightly so, and put pressure on him to resign. This brought out his "defense mode" as he pointed out that these were only charges, not a conviction, and that no students were involved nor did anything occur on school property. He hired two lawyers, one was criminal for his defense, and the other was civil to keep his job.

By December, when I learned he was dipping into our son's college fund, I knew I had to make a move, lest he drain all the small assets we had. Instead of waking up *from* a nightmare, as most do, it felt like I was waking up *to* a nightmare every morning. I look back at this period now, somewhat in awe, scarcely believing that I really did live through all of this turmoil. I was now living the cliché idea of having more inner strength than you think you have almost in robotic fashion. I contacted a lawyer and discreetly set things in motion which was difficult with him now being home most of the time. He was told by school district personnel to be home during school hours and to be available by home phone. By January he was served, and he was pretty amazed that I had pulled it off unbeknownst to him. I had to protect myself at this point.

The criminal court system in the small rural county moved very slowly, and he remained on paid leave for over a year and a half as we waited for an outcome. I could not exactly throw him out of the house not knowing what was going to happen, and we needed the financial stability of his income. He applied for jobs everywhere, but needless to say, in spite of his stellar career, no one wanted to touch him. He convinced himself and everyone else it was all a mistake, and that he was a victim of both the court system and school district personnel.

At one point we were informed that the media had gotten hold of the story, but thankfully it never came out....a true miracle. Through the court appearances I learned very little, and due to a technicality and a small town cop, who slipped up a few times, changing his story a bit, deals were made and his charges were reduced to a level that the school district had to accept. I will never fully know what transpired that night in the park, but there are too many facts I had gleaned from the paperwork I found for me to believe he was completely innocent. I pushed for him to start looking elsewhere to live.

By September 2008, he finally moved out, and a week later we were hit with Hurricane Ike resulting in major damage to our home. Fortunately my son and I were able to escape to my sister's home, where they had power. That week we also had the mediation session for the divorce, seated in separate rooms with our lawyers, to draw up an equitable plan for division of assets. Somehow I made it through, coping with extensive home repairs and insurance hassles by myself and wearily combing lists of home furnishings to be divided. It all seems so far in the past, though I remember the detail as if it were yesterday. The divorce was finalized later that month, and repairs to the house were underway.

In the spring of 2009, the school district decided in view of the lowered charges (now "disorderly conduct") it did not prevent him from being in the classroom. They would have him begin working as a substitute teacher while awaiting the final court outcome. I believe this was another attempt to get him to resign. He was sent to elementary schools and anything else they could think of that would be far from his comfort zone. It became a game, and he was determined to win. He mastered it all without complaint. That, paired with an effective lawyer, led to the school district being forced to offer him a full time position at a pretty difficult middle school for the upcoming school year where the head director was retiring. I am sure it would have been difficult to find a willing candidate to fill that position. This was a very lucky break for him, and he has just finished his second year there.

Meanwhile, I was trying to recover from so much. A divorce alone is life-changing, but when it involves these unique circumstances, a thick layer is added to the pile through which one must sort. It was not so much the "gay" part as the betrayal and lack of honesty that cut me to the core. I questioned everything in my mind, about him and about me, but found few answers.

Since the "incident" and haggling over assets, he was again cool and uncommunicative. There were so many new issues to be in charge of from finances to lawn mowing. I found bonding with others who have walked the same path was a tremendous help. As I moved forward and looked back, I began to write about the stages I walked and sometimes crawled through. This gave me a sense of accomplishment, to know that I really was coping, and that the darkest days could give way to better ones.

A year later, I had been coping with all of this long enough and could no longer be the keeper of his secret with my own kids. I just had to come clean with them over the real reasons for our divorce. My son had survived the trauma of all of this during his last years in high school and was now thriving in college; our daughter was successfully making it on her own. I had gained a lot of support through my correspondence with Bonnie Kaye, and with therapy and was "okay" with it all, enough to convince the kids that they need not worry over me. My now ex-husband felt otherwise and was petrified at the thought, and he tried desperately to convince me that they did not need to know.

Now more confident with myself, I assured him that they deserved the truth, and that I would stick to the facts, and leave out the details, and would not bash him. I was about to have major surgery and wanted to be sure they heard the real story just in case something happened. I carefully prepared, and the conversation went quite well. I had been warned by my "support group" that they might already have figured it out, but they, too, had no clue that their father was gay.

Being of the younger generation, they were rather accepting. In later conversations they stated that that was not the part that got them; it was the "abandonment" of workaholism and narcissistic ways throughout their childhoods that had alienated them from him the most. They both concluded that this must be kept to themselves, as they referenced the arrest and drama that ensued and how their friends would put it all together, resulting in a very difficult situation. I completely understood that it would be too much for them to deal with, with their friends, but it also saddened me that it had to be this way.

It is now four years since my discovery on that computer, and two and a half since the judge signed the official document, breaking our legal covenant. I have come a long way since that first shocking night in front of the computer. I have dealt with far more than I ever imagined I could or would ever have to. I have come to accept how my marriage came to be, and I wholeheartedly believe that my husband went into it without a conscious understanding of his homosexuality.

But I am so deeply hurt that he did not come clean with me when those feelings and urges surfaced. This was the ultimate betrayal of our vows. To continue to carry on with this deception, while your wife suffers in silence and depression and your children bear the fallout, is unspeakable. I believed so deeply in marriage for life, in commitment, in partnership, in mutual support, in having a "one and only" to love, and someone who would love me back equally. Yes, I had to get out of the marriage; there was never a doubt about that.

Even after working through so much in recovery, it is still painful to know and feel that I was part of something that failed, something that I believed in so strongly. For me, it took so long to actually get to the point of marriage, and then to have it all unravel so subtly and tragically year by year, has left me devastated at worst, and scarred at best; the sting (or burn) is still so destructive to the soul: "Should I ever believe in marriage again?" (The divorce rate is over 60% for 2nd marriages) "Do I deserve it?" "Will I ever trust anyone again?" "Will I ever trust myself?" "Can I ever risk falling for someone?" "What is meant for me?" "Am I too old to have "adolescent dreams"?" "How do you know if it will work?" My leap of faith last time didn't work out so well.

Because I can't share the whole truth with so many, I know they wonder what really happened: "What did Wendy do or not do to contribute to the demise of the marriage?" "It takes two, you know…" Then even now, I start to believe what they believe, that I must be flawed or have done something wrong or have not been *enough.* Because I can't share the whole truth, living here in the south, my friends (who are mostly well-intended), give me advice about moving forward, or think they understand something they will *never* understand. So these scars affect my friendships as well, and I have periods of feeling deep isolation, in spite of having friends and family surrounding me.

I do acknowledge often how grateful I am that he did not carry on while we were married or subject me to disease. I know this is not the case for many women in this circumstance, and I have great admiration for those who are coping with this on top of everything else.

I believe my ex husband has returned to the closet and locked the door given what he risked and put himself through. In a way makes it easier for me in that I don't have to watch him go off into the sunset with someone else, but it makes it harder for me to move on. He is now trying to become my "BFF," (Best Friend Forever) after mostly staying out of my life the first year or so after the divorce. I think he thought I would meet someone who would sweep me off my feet, and felt threatened by this. But now since it seems to be far from happening for me, and he is in denial as if nothing really "bad" ever happened, I guess he feels it's okay to call me, to "unload" about his happenings, primarily seeing himself as a victim in most of his circumstances, as he did for 20+ years in our marriage. In his eyes, I am still interested and will soothe him once again. Of course these calls begin under the guise of needing to communicate as co-parents, but quickly turn to being all about HIM! I am very careful not to engage him, offering nothing about my life and nothing more than an "uh-huh", but I am disappointed and frustrated that I let myself fall under this "spell" from time to time out of loneliness on my part.

A friend described it as having an old shoe that you just can't quite throw away yet. I must learn to just ignore him, but also feel the need to "keep him happy" for when financial issues arise concerning our college-aged son. I also wonder if deep down, I figure having him there, an arm's length away, is better than having NO ONE at all at this later stage of life. I have considered going back into therapy over this, as I have wrestled with it for a while, and seem to be stuck. I never believed people were meant to go through life alone, but here I am, again, and it still saddens me deeply. It's just so unfair for it to have come to this when I truly did nothing wrong but follow my heart. I need a partner to share life with, with whom to have a balance of give and take. I truly don't know if my scars will keep this from happening for me. I suppose my recovery process will always be that--a process.

In the end, in spite of the unexpected turns my life has taken, I have made it, thanks to so many who believed in and supported me even when they didn't know exactly what I was going through. Although I now have limited financial resources, I feel rich in my relationships with my family, friends and now adult children, who seem to be thriving. The rest of my journey is uncertain, but I do know that I possess the strength to survive it. Life is no longer about "happy endings" but about learning to appreciate all that is good along the way.

Conclusion

I would like to thank each of my wonderful contributors to this book who opened their hearts to our women by sharing their life stories. It takes a great deal of courage to sit down and write about your most personal and intimate moments and then share them with strangers. But these women did it to make sure that you would have the opportunity to feel connected to them and not feel so alone.

If you are a woman who is/was in a marriage to a gay man, I hope these stories have helped you as far as seeing that everything you are experiencing and feeling is "normal." Nothing else in your life may seem normal, but your feelings of despair, frustration, sadness, anger, and betrayal are. And guess what? For some women, it is the first time in a long time that the word "normal" can be used and make sense based on their Alice in Wonderland marriages where everything appears topsy-turvy.

There are no quick fixes to Gay Husband Recovery (GHR). I tell our women it is a process. For some it takes a year—for others a decade or more. The important thing to understand is that there is no set timeline for this process, and no one should make you feel pressured with statements of, "How long do you have to dwell on this? Get over it!" Recovery is based on your years of emotional and mental deterioration and how your husband supports you and the children now and in the future.

Several things I tell all of our women:

1. Do not feel like you have to do this alone. Write to me at Bonkaye@aol.com for support. I have a free monthly newsletter, support chats twice a week, an internet radio show at www.Blogtalkradio.com (type Straight Wives Talk Show into the bar on top) that you can access 24/7 with back episodes if you miss the live episodes on Sunday evenings live, and an annual face-to-face free healing weekend in Philadelphia,

Pennsylvania, in the autumn. You can also view my website at www.Gayhusbands.com for a list of additional resources and updated information.

2. Some women feel such a void after their marriages that they make the mistake and dive into a relationship when their marriages end. This is a big mistake because you are not ready for this. Work on rebuilding your own life during the first year so that you avoid repeating a mistake again by settling for less than what you deserve in your next relationship. There are lots of predators out there who are straight, and they are seeking women just like you—vulnerable, loving, and giving. I'll add low self-esteem to that list because most women have their self and sexual esteem registering at a very low point by the time their marriages end. Focus on rebuilding your life on your own before you find someone to help enhance it with you. You must be able to make yourself happy before thinking about someone to share it with. You can never count on any man to be the primary source of your happiness or you will end up in the same place you are running away from. However, you can still have fun and practice, practice, practice until your soulmate shows up.

3. Accept that there was nothing you could do to save your marriage to a gay man. You didn't make him gay—you couldn't stop him from being gay either. He was born gay. At what point his homosexuality surfaced is the issue. No one knows when or how that happens—but it does.

4. Be role models to your children. Children are destined to repeat your patterns—it is called learned behavior or what I refer to as the "monkey see, monkey do, monkey act just like you" syndrome. If your children see that you have stayed in an unfulfilling marriage, chances are they will stay in one too when they get married. If they see a lack of emotion or passion in your marriage, they will think that this is the norm

and find someone who will offer them just as little as you have been receiving. Remember—it is better to come from a broken home than to live in one. Children suffer greatly in these marriages seeing the unhappiness of their parents. Often they know what is happening before their mothers do. They become the "keeper of the secret" for their fathers which tears them apart with guilt and anxiety. No one doubts your love for the children. Put their emotional health first.

5. Feel free to vent your anger because you will be angry. But at some point, you have to let it go before it turns to bitterness. Bitterness destroys you and your children—not your husband. Part of moving through anger is "acceptance" of the situation. You don't have to forgive unless the forgiveness is earned, but you can learn to accept that it is what it is so you can move on and take back your own life. I also believe that forgiveness must be earned; otherwise, you will not have closure for yourself. A husband can "earn" your forgiveness by acknowledging your pain and making sure he is there to give you the needed supports after the marriage.

6. We have many happily ever again stories. Women move on and sometimes find their real soulmate. Don't give up on love if that is what you want. Some women are happy to be alone on their own, and that's fine. But for those of you who want a new relationship, go looking for it because it's out there looking for you!

Finally--**learn my mantra and repeat it a dozen times a day until you believe it:**

<u>Life was never meant to be this complicated. Period.</u>

With love and hope,
Bonnie ♥

CPSIA information can be obtained at www.ICGtesting.com
Printed in the USA
LVOW060533280911

248204LV00002B/59/P